COMPREHENSIVE RESEARCH
AND STUDY GUIDE

Mark Strand

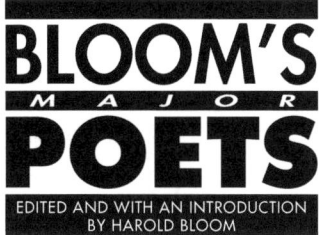

BLOOM'S
MAJOR
POETS
EDITED AND WITH AN INTRODUCTION
BY HAROLD BLOOM

CURRENTLY AVAILABLE

BLOOM'S MAJOR POETS

Maya Angelou
Elizabeth Bishop
William Blake
Gwendolyn Brooks
Robert Browning
Geoffrey Chaucer
Samuel Taylor Coleridge
Hart Crane
E.E. Cummings
Dante
Emily Dickinson
John Donne
H.D.
T.S. Eliot
Robert Frost
Seamus Heaney
Homer
A.E. Housman
Langston Hughes
John Keats
John Milton
Sylvia Plath
Edgar Allan Poe
Poets of World War I
Shakespeare's Poems & Sonnets
Percy Shelley
Wallace Stevens
Mark Strand
Alfred, Lord Tennyson
Walt Whitman
William Carlos Williams
William Wordsworth
William Butler Yeats

COMPREHENSIVE RESEARCH
AND STUDY GUIDE

Mark Strand

CHELSEA HOUSE
PUBLISHERS
A Haights Cross Communications Company
Philadelphia

BLOOM'S
MAJOR
POETS
EDITED AND WITH AN INTRODUCTION
BY HAROLD BLOOM

© 2003 by Chelsea House Publishers, a subsidiary of
Haights Cross Communications.

A Haights Cross Communications Company

Introduction © 2003 by Harold Bloom.

All rights reserved. No part of this publication may be reproduced
or transmitted in any form or by any means without the written
permission of the publisher.

Printed and bound in the United States of America.

First Printing
1 3 5 7 9 8 6 4 2

Library of Congress Cataloging-in-Publication Data

Mark Strand / Harold Bloom, ed..
   p. cm. — (Bloom's major poets)
Includes bibliographical references and index.
  ISBN 0-7910-7393-9
  1. Strand, Mark, 1934——Criticism and interpretation. I. Bloom,
Harold. II. Series.
  PS3569.T69 Z78 2002
  811'.54—dc21

Chelsea House Publishers
1974 Sproul Road, Suite 400
Broomall, PA 19008-0914
http://www.chelseahouse.com

Contributing Editor: Camille-Yvette Welsch

Cover design by Keith Trego

Layout by EJB Publishing Services

CONTENTS

User's Guide	7
About the Editor	8
Editor's Note	9
Introduction	10
Biography of Mark Strand	14
Critical Analysis of "The Story of Our Lives"	17
Critical Views on "The Story of Our Lives"	21
Linda Gregerson on Narrative Structure in the Poem	21
Thomas McClanahan on the Act of Creation within the Poem	23
Peter Stitt on the Transubstantiation of Thought to Word to Reality	24
John Bensko on the Agency of Art in Reflexive Narration	25
David Kirby on Dealing with the Ideal State	28
Sven Birkerts on the Lack of Telos in Strand's Poetry	32
Critical Analysis of "The Way It Is"	33
Critical Views on "The Way It Is"	37
Richard Howard on the Poet's Movement from Interior Dreamscape to Public Place	37
Harold Bloom on the Poem as Representative of a Shift in Strand's Poetics	38
Peter Stitt on the Poem as an Attempt to Define the World	40
Critical Analysis of "Elegy for My Father"	42
Critical Views on "Elegy for My Father"	46
Laurence Lieberman on the Use of Litany	46
Richard Howard on the Poem as an Affirmation of Life	48
David Kirby on the Poem as Loss of Self	50
Sven Birkerts on the Poem's Influences	53
Edward Byrne on the Poem as a Precursor to *A Blizzard of One*	55

Critical Analysis of "Dark Harbor" 57
Critical Views on "Dark Harbor" 62
   Christopher Benfey on the Poem as a Kind of Ars
     Poetica 62
   David St. John on the Use of Dream and Memory 64
   David Lehman on the Thematic Influence of
     Wallace Stevens 65
   Jeffrey Donaldson on the Use of the Orpheus Myth 68
   Richard Tillinghast on Strand's Use of and Place
     Within the Western Canon 72
   Christopher R. Miller on the Comparison between
     Dark Harbor and Stevens' "Waving Adieu, Adieu,
     Adieu" 73
   James F. Nicosia: Marsyas in *Dark Harbor* 76

Works By Mark Strand 85
Works About Mark Strand 87
Acknowledgments 91
Index of Themes and Ideas 93

USER'S GUIDE

This volume is designed to present biographical, critical, and bibliographical information on the author and the author's best-known or most important poems. Following Harold Bloom's editor's note and introduction is a concise biography of the author that discusses major life events and important literary accomplishments. A critical analysis of each poem follows, tracing significant themes, patterns, and motifs in the work. As with any study guide, it is recommended that the reader read the poem beforehand, and have a copy of the poem being discussed available for quick reference.

A selection of critical extracts, derived from previously published material, follows each thematic analysis. In most cases, these extracts represent the best analysis available from a number of leading critics. Because these extracts are derived from previously published material, they will include the original notations and references when available. Each extract is cited, and readers are encouraged to check the original publication as they continue their research. A bibliography of the author's writings, a list of additional books and articles on the author and their work, and an index of themes and ideas conclude the volume.

ABOUT THE EDITOR

Harold Bloom is Sterling Professor of the Humanities at Yale University and Henry W. and Albert A. Berg Professor of English at the New York University Graduate School. He is the author of over 20 books, and the editor of more than 30 anthologies of literary criticism.

Professor Bloom's works include *Shelley's Mythmaking* (1959), *The Visionary Company* (1961), *Blake's Apocalypse* (1963), *Yeats* (1970), *A Map of Misreading* (1975), *Kabbalah and Criticism* (1975), *Agon: Toward a Theory of Revisionism* (1982), *The American Religion* (1992), *The Western Canon* (1994), and *Omens of Millennium: The Gnosis of Angels, Dreams, and Resurrection* (1996). *The Anxiety of Influence* (1973) sets forth Professor Bloom's provocative theory of the literary relationships between the great writers and their predecessors. His most recent books include *Shakespeare: The Invention of the Human*, a 1998 National Book Award finalist, *How to Read and Why* (2000), and *Genius: A Mosiac of One Hundred Exemplary Creative Minds* (2002).

Professor Bloom earned his Ph.D. from Yale University in 1955 and has served on the Yale faculty since then. He is a 1985 MacArthur Foundation Award recipient and served as the Charles Eliot Norton Professor of Poetry at Harvard University in 1987–88. In 1999 he was awarded the prestigious American Academy of Arts and Letters Gold Medal for Criticism. Professor Bloom is the editor of several other Chelsea House series in literary criticism, including BLOOM'S MAJOR SHORT STORY WRITERS, BLOOM'S MAJOR NOVELISTS, BLOOM'S MAJOR DRAMATISTS, BLOOM'S MODERN CRITICAL INTERPRETATIONS, BLOOM'S MODERN CRITICAL VIEWS, and BLOOM'S BIOCRITIQUES.

EDITOR'S NOTE

This volume offers critical views on four major poems by Mark Strand: *The Story of Our Lives*, *The Way It Is*, *Elegy for my Father* and *Dark Harbor*.

My Introduction comments upon *Dark Harbor*, and attempts to unravel the intricate relations between Strand and Wallace Stevens.

There is so high a quality of commentary throughout that it is invidious to single out individual critics.

On *The Story of Our Lives* I find Linda Gregerson and Sven Birkerts most illuminating.

Richard Howard comments brilliantly on Strand's exteriorization in *The Way it Is*.

On the dark *Elegy for My Father*, I am particularly moved by Richard Howard and Sven Birkerts again.

Dark Harbor is most searchingly explored by James Nicosia in his adumbrations of the figure of Marysas.

INTRODUCTION
Harold Bloom

I have known Mark Strand, as person and as poet, for more than half a century. His gift is harbored rather than sparse: that is my interpretation of his major work to date, *Dark Harbor: A Poem* (1993). The poem constitutes a "Proem" and forty-five cantos or sections.

Dark Harbor, like some earlier poems by Strand, is an overt homage to Wallace Stevens. It is as though casting aside anxieties of influences Strand wishes reconcilement with his crucial precursor. The "Proem" sets forth vigorously: "The burning/Will of weather, blowing overhead, would be his muse." But, by Canto IV, we are in the world of Stevens:

> There is a certain triviality in living here,
> A lightness, a comic monotony that one tries
> To undermine with shows of energy, a devotion
>
> To the vagaries of desire, whereas over there
> Is a seriousness, a stiff, inflexible gloom
> That shrouds the disappearing soul, a weight
>
> That shames our lightness. Just look
> Across the river and you will discover
> How unworthy you are as you describe what you see,
>
> Which is bound by what is available.
> On the other side, no one is looking this way.
> They are committed to obstacles,
>
> To the textures and levels of darkness,
> To the tedious enactment of duration.
> And they labor not for bread or love
>
> But to perpetuate the balance between the past
> And the future. They are the future as it
> Extends itself, just as we are the past

> Coming to terms with itself. Which is why
> The napkins are pressed, and the cookies have come
> On time, and why the glass of milk, looking so chic
>
> In its whiteness, begs us to sip. None of this happens
> Over there. Relief from anything is seen
> As timid, a sign of shallowness or worse.

This is the voice of the master, particularly in *An Ordinary Evening in New Haven*. Strand shrewdly undoes Stevens to the glass of milk, setting aside any more metaphysical concerns. An effort is made, for fifteen cantos, to domesticate Stevens, but the great voice, of Stevens and Strand fused together, returns in Canto XVI:

> It is true, as someone has said, that in
> A world without heaven all is farewell.
> Whether you wave your hand or not,
>
> It is farewell, and if no tears come to your eyes
> It is still farewell, and if you pretend not to notice,
> Hating what passes, it is still farewell.
>
> Farewell no matter what. And the palms as they lean
> Over the green, bright lagoon, and the pelicans
> Diving, and the listening bodies of bathers resting,
>
> Are stages in an ultimate stillness, and the movement
> Of sand, and of wind, and the secret moves of the body
> Are part of the same, a simplicity that turns being
>
> Into an occasion for mourning, or into an occasion
> Worth celebrating, for what else does one do,
> Feeling the weight of the pelicans' wings,
>
> The density of the palms' shadows, the cells that darken
> The backs of bathers? These are beyond the distortions
> Of chance, beyond the evasions of music. The end
>
> Is enacted again and again. And we feel it
> In the temptations of sleep, in the moon's ripening,
> In the wine as it waits in the glass.

It is Stevens who tells us that, without heaven, all farewells are final. What enchants me here are the Strandian variations on farewell. Waves and tears yield to very Stevensian palms, and to the pelicans of Florida, venereal soil. A greater meditation, suitable to Strand and Stevens as seers of the weather, arrives in Canto XXIV:

> Now think of the weather and how it is rarely the same
> For any two people, how when it is small, precision is needed
> To say when it is really an aura or odor or even an air
>
> Of certainty, or how, as the hours go by, it could be thought of
> As large because of the number of people it touches.
> Its strength is something else: tornados are small
>
> But strong and cloudless summer days seem infinite
> But tend to be weak since we don't mind being out in them.
> Excuse me, is this the story of another exciting day,
>
> The sort of thing that accompanies preparations for dinner?
> Then what say we talk about the inaudible-the shape it assumes,
> And what social implications it holds,
>
> Or the somber flourishes of autumn-the bright
> Or blighted leaves falling, the clicking of cold branches,
> The new color of the sky, its random blue.

Is that final tercet Strand or Stevens? As the sequence strengthens, deliberate echoes of Josh Ashbery, Octavio Paz and Wordworth are evoked by Strand, until he achieves a grand apotheosis in his final canto:

> I am sure you would find it misty here,
> With lots of stone cottages badly needing repair.
> Groups of souls, wrapped in cloaks, sit in the fields
>
> Or stroll the winding unpaved roads. They are polite,
> And oblivious to their bodies, which the wind passes through,
> Making a shushing sound. Not long ago,
>
> I stopped to rest in a place where an especially
> Thick mist swirled up from the river. Someone,
> Who claimed to have known me years before,

Approached, saying there were many poets
Wandering around who wished to be alive again.
They were ready to say the words they had been unable to say-

Words whose absence had been the silence of love,
Of pain, and even of pleasure. Then he joined a small group,
Gathered beside a fire. I believe I recognized

Some of the faces, but as I approached they tucked
Their heads under their wings. I looked away to the hills
Above the river, where the golden lights of sunset

And sunrise are one and the same, and saw something flying
Back and forth, fluttering its wings. Then it stopped in mid-air.
It was an angel, one of the good ones, about to sing.

The aura is Dante's, and we are in a spooky place, paradise of poets or purgatory of poets. If one line above all others in *Dark Harbor* reverberates within me, it is: "They were ready to say the words they had been unable to say-" The accent remains late Stevens, but with a difference is altogether Mark Strand's.

BIOGRAPHY OF
Mark Strand

Mark Strand published his first book in 1964, the year he turned thirty. In the years following, he tackled poetry as a translator, critic, and poet influenced by writers like Borges, Stevens, Bishop, Kafka, and Donald Justice. As an editor and translator, he exposed American readers to South American poets, the intricacies of form, and his notions on the essential aspects of poetry in translation. Always amiable, Strand is sought after for interviews, bringing the unique perspective of an artist who has experimented in different genres, dabbling in fiction, non-fiction, scholarly critique, children's books and painting as well as poetry.

Born in Summerside, Prince Edward Island, Canada, on April 11, 1934, Mark Strand spent much of his youth relocating across North and South America due to his father's job as a salesman. The family lived in Cuba, Columbia, Peru, Mexico, Philadelphia, Halifax, and Montreal, affording the young boy exposure to a number of languages, although at the time his primary interest was not poetry, but painting. The dream of being an artist lasted until he was twenty.

Strand attended Antioch College and completed his BA in 1957. By 1959, he had completed a BFA at Yale, studying under Joseph Albers. During his course of study, he also took English classes and excelled in them, and perhaps most formatively, he kept returning to the poems of Wallace Stevens. While at Yale, Strand received the Cook Prize and the Bergin Prize, and came to the realization that he was not to be a painter, rather, he would become a poet. In 1960, he received a Fulbright scholarship to Italy to study nineteenth century poetry. Upon Strand's return to the United States, he married a fellow Fulbright scholar whom he had met in Italy, Antonia Ratensky, in 1961 and began to be published in *The New Yorker*. That same year, he began his study at the University of Iowa, under the guidance of Donald Justice with whom he studied for one year, earning his MA. After completing his degree, he began a three-year teaching stint at the

University of Iowa. In 1964, he published his first book of poetry, *Sleeping with One Eye Open*, and though it received little to no critical fanfare, it does provide the symbolic apparatus for reading Strand's work. The book foreshadows his darkness, the tension in his characters, the search for self and identity, the grotesque detail, the morbid humor, the dream-like, elegant tone. It also introduced a certain cavalier cleverness and empty, formal ease for which some critics have chastised him.

After the publication of his book, Strand left Iowa to teach as a Fulbright Lecturer in Brazil. During his time there, he occasionally saw Elizabeth Bishop and began gathering information for translating Carlos Drummond de Andrade, a Brazilian poet whose poetry shares a keen feeling of isolation with Strand's. Funded by an Ingram-Merrill grant, Strand returned to the United States and took up residence in New York City. He began taking a series of teaching jobs at various colleges and universities, Mt. Holyoke, the University of Washington, Columbia, Yale, Princeton, Brandeis, University of Virginia, Wesleyan, and Harvard. In 1967, he was awarded an NEA grant and, in 1968, editor Harry Ford accepted and published Strand's second book, *Reasons for Moving: Poems*. Strand claims Ford as the reason he has a career in poetry, and when Ford left Atheneum in favor of Knopf, Strand went with him.

Reasons for Moving continued to have a feeling of barely contained fear, an intense questioning of what constitutes the self, and a sense of self-negation. In these poems, Strand's speakers often move between a world of their own making and the world-at-large, each with its own uneasy atmosphere often told in images juxtaposing frantic activity with absolute stillness. After receiving a Rockefeller Foundation Grant in 1968, Strand continued working, and by 1970, he published another collection, *Darker*, that met with critical acceptance. Many believed the book to be the start of a more life affirming oeuvre for Strand, although the book retains his fascination with the divided self. In 1973, he published *The Story of Our Lives*, his most critically praised book at that time, which marked a turning point. The poems were longer, more narrative and more autobiographical than his earlier poems, although they are still driven by Strand's obsession with the interior and the way in which the imagination figures reality. He received the first Edgar Allan Poe award from the Academy of American Poets in 1974. The honors kept coming: he received awards from the National Institute for Arts and Letters and an American Academy Award in Literature as well as a Guggenheim Fellowship in 1975. His fifth major collection appeared in 1978, *The Late Hour*.

Strand also found the 1970s to be intensely productive as a translator and editor, working with Charles Simic and Octavio Paz on two of his projects. The work brought much of Strand's idiosyncratic taste to the market, exposing more people to the influence of European and South American poets. In 1980, Strand published his *Selected Poems*, his only volume of poetry during the decade. Instead of poetry, he focused his energies on children's books, fiction, prose, and art criticism—publishing six volumes collectively. He received critical praise for his prose although the response to his children's books was mixed. In the 1990's, Strand made a triumphant return to poetry, serving as the United States Poet Laureate from 1990-1991, and publishing *The Continuous Life* in 1990, a book length poem and winner of Yale University's Bollingen Prize, *Dark Harbor* in 1993, and his Boston Book Review Bingham Poetry Prize and Pulitzer Prize winning volume, *Blizzard of One* in 1993. Critical praise was overwhelming. Writers and scholars claimed that this was Strand writing at his best, with a fully developed voice and balance they had not seen before.

In the year 2000, success continued. Strand co-edited *The Making of a Poem: A Norton Anthology of Poetic Forms* and a book of essays *The Weather of Words: Poetic Inventions*. He currently teaches on the Committee for Social Thought at the University of Chicago as the Andrew MacLeish Distinguished Service Professor of Social Thought. Ultimately, his contribution to American poetry has been vast. As an essayist, his writing is insightful, funny and informative. In translating, his ear is keen and his taste impeccable. But, it is as a poet that he is most influential, attacking throughout his poetry the question of the self and its divisions and tensions, and the place of the poet and poetry in the contemporary world.

CRITICAL ANALYSIS OF
"The Story of Our Lives"

This title poem from Strand's fourth book reveals a structural shift in his poetry, marking a book of lengthier narrative poems. As with much of Strand's work, the struggle of the poem is both internal and external. The characters cannot help themselves, trapped by their own inertia and inability to walk away from expectations both societal and personal. The poem questions the notion of self and how it is created through story and action.

The poem begins with a couple who are "reading the story of our lives / which takes place in a room." Immediately, Strand gives his major plot point and suggests the kind of lives these two are leading: small and self-contained, fitting neatly into one room. And though the room has a view of the street, as in many of Strand's poems, no one is there; nothing stirs. Instead, a dream-like, or death-like, hush prevails, the furniture never moves and everything becomes slowly darker. It seems as if the poem happens underwater with its slow pace, muffled sounds and ever-falling darkness. Indeed, the moment when all is quiet, where the leaves are full, is reminiscent of Keats's urn, a momentary, inalterable beauty and ripeness. Still, even this moment, which the speaker claims as ideal, is flawed. The speaker admits "We keep turning the pages, / hoping for something, / something like mercy or change, /" Both the husband/speaker and his wife desire something more than the set life the book has given them, but with a sad irony that is typical of Strand, that desire is thwarted. They are unable, either separately or together, to ruin this perceived ideal story and state, and so they become what they fear, stagnant and over-ripe, spoiled and painfully aware of themselves, their story, their failures, their future.

In the second section, they are still reading the story of their lives. Strand uses the first person point of view throughout the poem to suggest that, as readers, we are in some small way mirroring the actions of the couple, particularly the speaker. The story unfolds while we read it, as it unfolds for the narrator. The repetition of the phrase "We are reading the story of our lives" suggests that the action is cyclical and constant. The speaker claims they read "as though we were in it, / as though we had written it." Here, the idea of the speaker and his wife feeling distanced from the book is integral. They still believe themselves to be more than the story the book suggests. They still believe they have choices, that they might escape the pull of this knowledge. In many ways, the story suggests a reverse Tree of Knowledge; the fruit consumed does not provide knowledge of mortality, instead it offers the speaker his life and all of his choices. The knowledge is paralyzing. The speaker wonders again and again who is writing the story; he knows only that he is not the primary mover in this story. He tries briefly to turn from the book. He tries to create causality based on his own decisions; he chooses to try and write the story himself believing that the act of writing will give him some autonomy. Before he can get very far, the book tells him he put his pen down. This preternatural accuracy unsettles the speaker and defeats him. He turns to watch his wife read the book, knowing that she has come to the section where she falls in love with the neighbor. He tells her "You fell in love with him / because you knew that he would never visit you, / would never know you were waiting." After reading the story of her life with the speaker, the woman chooses ignorance. She chooses a man who will never know what she wants. She prefers the anonymity and the free will it affords her.

As she reads, the narrator watches her, allegedly imagining his life without her. She looks up from the book with this knowledge. It rends the already growing rift between them. The speaker writes, "The book describes much more than it should. / It wants to divide us." In writing this, the speaker bestows power upon the book; it is a power neither he nor his wife possesses. With a life already described, and in such unforgiving detail, the characters lose their motivation to live that life and stagnate in their room.

The third section begins with the husband waking and internalizing the notion that he has no life, only the story of it. When the wife disagrees, he points to the book, showing her where she disagreed. She turns back to sleep, her last refuge for the unexpected and the speaker continues to read, reliving the moments that the wife used to find exciting, the moments before she had all the knowledge that the book provided. The husband turns to the early part of their relationship and relishes the sense of uncertainty that was there. In response the book claims, "*In those moments it was his book. / A bleak crown rested uneasily on his head. / He was the brief ruler of inner and outer discord, / anxious in his own kingdom.*" The book intimates that this man could never actually rule his own life. His anxiety would overwhelm him, as it overwhelms him now when all of the events are written before him. He is paralyzed by his own fears; he both fears and desires the idea that something unexpected might happen, for the good or the bad.

He continues reading, despite these fears, or perhaps because of them. He finds that his wife sleeps to slip back in time, and for a moment, he wants to inhabit that sleep with her, to escape the all-knowing book. The book chronicles this desire, stealing from it all of his tenderness:

> *He wanted to see her naked and vulnerable,*
> *To see her in the refuse, the costumes and masks*
> *Of unattainable state.*
> *It was as if he were drawn*
> *Irresistibly to failure.*

After reading this devastating portrayal of himself, the speaker finds it hard to continue reading. He tries to move away from the prescribed action, relying instead on his old form of knowledge and story telling. He watches his wife's face and breathing and tries to read her that way, to understand and read signs of his own volition, to attribute her actions and thoughts to a motivation that cannot be recognized by the book.

The speaker cannot keep it up though. He goes back to the book, searching for a perfect moment to live in, all the time knowing that it is an impossible feat. Throughout, he knows that his only chance at a perfect moment is to destroy the book, but he cannot do it; he needs to have its corrupting power. The section ends with one of the poem's most devastating lines: "It never explains. It only reveals." And, the revelation is ugly and sordid, inconsiderate of motivation and history. Instead, it runs as a relentless, shallow newsreel, images devoid of context. The lack of context ultimately becomes dehumanizing.

In prolonged agony, the couple continues to view the book. They stare at themselves in the mirror, as if reading the book, watching themselves in reverse to keep from being lonely. They need to begin speaking to each other, to rectify the wrongs. The book says so. It even acknowledges its own complicity in destroying this relationship. Instead of speaking, they turn to the book and more stagnation. In the book and in the room that is their world, everything becomes make-believe and their own pain is suspect because nothing has actually happened. There is nothing to reconcile save imagined wrongs told by the book.

The last section affirms all the hopelessness that has come before. "The book will not survive." Of course not—it is a representation of two mortal people. The tale necessarily ends. The room continues to darken, adding to the mood of desperation. The speaker cannot put the book aside; he wants to and does not want to. His indecision binds him ultimately to a life of nothing. Bound with him is his wife. They live inside the book and learn to accept the truth of their lives: "They are the book and they are / nothing else." Here, Strand's careful line break supports the struggle of the poem. He acknowledges that they exist, i.e. "they are" but that their existence means nothing. They remain caught in a limbo of indecision. Should they break from expectation and this prescribed notion of their lives and this very dangerous book that tells them how to live and warns them of what is to come, or should they make their own decisions, live without its corrupting power and fear living without knowing what will happen, without being able to prepare? It underscores one of the pervasive fears in Strand's work, a notion of nothingness and how we help to create for ourselves through our own fears, indecision and inaction.

CRITICAL VIEWS ON
"The Story of Our Lives"

Linda Gregerson on Narrative Structure in the Poem

[Linda Gregerson is a Professor at the University of Michigan and a poet. She has three books of poems, the most recent entitled, *Waterborne*. In this essay, she examines the notion of negation in Strand's work and its evolution through the structuring of his poems.]

As the poet moves further away from his earliest poems, the tension between line break and phrasing softens, enjambment nearly disappears. The simplest of syntactical patterns simply repeat; the eddies and stills of imagery even out. The poems encounter less and less resistance as they move down the page, until their progress becomes as frictionless as that of a kite or a ghost ship:

> We are reading the story of our lives
> which takes place in a room.
> The room looks out on a street.
> There is no one there,
> no sound of anything.
>   ("The Story of Our Lives")

"The Story of Our Lives" and "The Untelling," centerpieces of Strand's fourth major collection, pursue the formal discoveries made in "The Kite." Each poem contains a story that contains a poem that steadily dismantles containment. As "The Story of Our Lives" proceeds, a man and a woman, side by side, consult the course of love in a book. Though love unfolds and doubles back, no point of origin or terminus appears, no point, that is, beyond which the mind might firmly declare itself to be outside the story:

The book never discusses the causes of love.
It claims confusion is a necessary good.
It never explains. It only reveals.

In this way the book preserves the reasons for moving:

It describes your dependence on desire,
how the momentary disclosures
of purpose make you afraid.

Books have promulgated desire before. When Paolo and Francesca, side by side, read the story of Lancelot and Guinevere, adulterous love renewed its kingdom: "A Gallehault was the book and he who wrote it; that day we read no farther in it" (*Inferno* V, 137–38). Gallehault served as a go-between for Lancelot and Guinevere. Boccaccio subtitled *The Decameron* "Prince Gallehault" and dedicated his book to *otiose donne*, idle ladies. The pattern for seduction is perfectly explicit, and perfectly vicarious. Strand's own poems mediate a vast inherited culture by appearing to build in a clearing. Their faithlessness is part of their pedigree, its faithlessness is the cement of love. Paolo and Francesca owed their fealty and their desire to Gianciotto, Lancelot and Guinevere to Arthur. The man and the woman on the couch must interpolate a breach of faith in order to perfect desire:

I lean back and watch you read
about the man across the street.
....
You fell in love with him
because you knew that he would never visit you,
Would never know you were waiting.
Night after night you would say
that he was like me.

—Linda Gregerson. "Negative Capability." *Negative Capability: Contemporary American Poetry* (Ann Arbor, University of Michigan Press, 2001.): pp. 5–29. Originally appeared in *Parnassus: Poetry in Review* 9:2 (1981): 90–114.

Thomas McClanahan on the Act of Creation within the Poem

[Dr. Thomas McClanahan serves as the Associate Vice President for Grants and Research for the South Carolina Arts Council. Here, he discusses the way in which Strand uses poetry/the act of creation as a mode for understanding his reality.]

In *The Story of Our Lives* (1973), Strand attempts to come to terms with reality through the imagination. Much like the woman in Wallace Steven's "The Idea of Order at Key West" who must "order words of the sea," Strand's persona in "To Begin" creates a world out of emptiness. It is an effort at imagining a world into existence: "He stared at the ceiling / and imagined his breath shaping itself into words." The poet figure forces himself to say words that, in turn, will prefigure a real world. The process is slow and uncertain. It is ephemeral and unordered, but it is an essential step in the direction of poetic and metaphysical order:

> In the dark he would still be uncertain about how to begin.
> He would mumble to himself; he would follow
> his words to learn where he was.
> He would begin.
> And the room, the house, the field,
> the woods beyond the field, would also begin,
> and in the sound of his own voice beginning
> he would hear them.

But even this successful creation is short-lived because Strand understands that we must create and recreate endlessly if we are to maintain this reality. In "The Story of Our Lives," Strand clearly points to this need for continual creation. In the second part of the poem, he reinforces the notion that we fashion our own existences through our imaginations:

> We are reading the story of our lives
> as though we were in it,
> as though we had written it.

But all must face the pessimistic knowledge that "The book will not survive. / We are the living proof of that. / It is dark outside, / in the room it is darker."

"The Untelling" picks up where "The Story of Our Lives" concludes. The poet figure's attempt to give relatives an account of a day he has recently spent with them illustrates the pain and inherent inaccuracy of any effort to chronicle truth. The more the man tries to describe what he believes has taken place, the more paralyzed he becomes:

> His pursuit was a form of evasion:
> the more he tried to uncover
> the more there was to conceal
> the less he understood.
> If he kept it up,
> he would lose everything.

His attempts to "uncover" meet with failure, and the poem concludes with the poet beginning once again to write it. Unlike the situation in "To Begin," where the poet has no objective experience from which to fashion his story, the poet figure in "The Untelling" has all the objective reality he can stand. His problem is that of selectivity, not creation from nothing, and it becomes apparent that the anguish of fashioning truth from reality is as real for Strand as the pain of making a poem out of the raw material of subjective consciousness.

—Thomas McClanahan, "Mark Strand." *Dictionary of Literary Biography, Volume 5: American Poets Since World War II, First Series.* Ed. Donald J. Greiner. Gale, 1980.

PETER STITT ON THE TRANSUBSTANTIATION OF THOUGHT TO WORD TO REALITY

[Peter Stitt is the Editor of *The Gettysburg Review* and a full professor of English at Gettysburg College. He is a prolific reviewer and the author of *Uncertainty and Plenitude: Five Contemporary Poets* and *The World's Hieroglyphic Beauty: Five American Poets*. In this review, he articulates Strand's method of internalizing the world to the point where it becomes a separate written reality for the speaker in the poem.]

The point of such poems as this is to strip away the outer world so as to make the subject of poetry the act of perception in the mind, the creation of the poem on the page. At a slightly later stage in the development of this type of poetry (in which the theme is the method, the method the theme) the version of reality created on the page can come back and determine the course of reality in the world. Which is precisely what happens in "The Story of Our Lives," where the action of the poem is defined early: "We are reading the story of our lives / which takes place in a room." Mark Strand is, in many ways, a latter-day symbolist, though his system is neither elaborate nor especially consistent. Of the significance of one image, however, we can be relatively sure—when he sets a poem in "a room," he means that room to stand for the mental world, as becomes clear later in this poem: "It is almost as if the room were the world. / We sit beside each other on the couch, / reading about the couch. / We say it is ideal. / It is ideal." To think something in this poem is to write it; and to think it or to write it is to make it part of reality, an event in the world or the room. Thus, "We are reading the story of our lives / as though we were in it, / as though we had written it." Precisely. And in the final stage: "This morning I woke and believed / there was no more to our lives / than the story of our lives. / When you disagreed, I pointed / to the place in the book where you disagreed."

—Peter Stitt. "Stages of Reality: The Mind/Body Problem in Contemporary Poetry." *The Georgia Review* 37: 1 (Spring 1983): 201–210.

JOHN BENSKO ON THE AGENCY OF ART IN REFLEXIVE NARRATION

[John Bensko is an Assistant Professor of English at the University of Memphis. He is the author of three books of poetry and his fiction has appeared in *Quarterly West* and *The Georgia Review*, among other journals. Here, he examines the way in which reflexive narration creates for art the power of agency of the lives of the characters in the poem.]

The structure of narrative, therefore, has within it an unsynthesizable analog of the relationship between man and his experience. But narrative realism tries to give the illusion of the unchangeable primacy of the *fabula*, and this limits the poet and the reader not just artistically, but philosophically and psychologically as well. Reflexivity, on the other hand, allows the poet to maintain the unsynthesizable quality of the relation between art and reality and to explore the interchange. In Mark Strand's title poem from *The Story of Our Lives* (25–31), for example, the narrator reads from a book which tells the story of him and his wife:

> In one of the chapters
> I lean back and push the book aside
> because the book says
> it is what I am doing.
> I lean back and begin to write about the book.
> I write that I wish to move beyond the book,
> beyond my life into another life.
> I put the pen down.
> The book says: *He put the pen down*
> *and turned and watched her reading*
> *the part about herself falling in love.*
> The book is more accurate than we can imagine.

The title, "The Story of Our Lives," suggests an autobiography, but Strand inverts the common relationship of *fabula* to *sjuzhet*, making the plot of the book control what is supposed to be the preeminent reality of their lives. The "book" becomes the embodiment of a truthfulness which exposes more of the reality than the narrator wishes to know, and we wonder: is the art of the book true to reality; or is it the result of an overly intense confessional compulsion which has a mind of its own and is creating the aesthetic pleasures of painful emotions? Has art, in other words, become an agent on its own, transforming our lives, mediating between the reality of our feelings and our awareness of them in order to create forms and significances which are its own, determined as much by the necessities of art as by those of the human truth. One might say that such questions are far-fetched, and that Strand is indulging needlessly in a fantasy; but his poem confronts serious questions about the confessional poetry of the recent decades: how often do the needs of art dictate that the poet develop some area of suffering, and how often does actual suffering result in art? Does writing about one's own life restrict that life or become a way of exploring and broadening it? Speaking to his wife, the narrator says of the book:

> It describes your dependence on desire,
> how the momentary disclosures
> of purpose make you afraid.
> The book describes more than it should.
> It wants to divide us.

Strand projects a kind of aesthetic determinism which rules their lives. At the end of the poem, the book's narration takes over from the human narrator, narrating its own story as well:

> *They sat beside each other on the couch.*
> *They were determined to accept the truth.*
> *Whatever it was they would accept it.*
> *The book would have to be written*
> *and would have to be read.*
> *They are the book and they are*
> *nothing else.*

By merging the protagonists and the story of the protagonists, the poem multiplies our perspectives on the experience, creating aesthetic distance and also destroying that distance. The reflexivity allows Strand to objectify psychological processes which are artistic but also are intimately connected with our lives. Because the reflexive narration breaks up the experience and reflects the perspectives of subject and subject-as-artifice on each other, it expands the poetic space of the narrational surface.

The *fabula-sjuzhet* division becomes much more than a structural device for critics; it is the embodiment of the complex, diverging, and yet inseparable elements of the determinism of natural events, the human will, and the imagination.

—John Bensko. "Reflexive Narration in Contemporary American Poetry." *The Journal of Narrative Theory* 16:2 (Spring 1986): pp. 81–96.

DAVID KIRBY ON DEALING WITH THE IDEAL STATE

[David Kirby, author or co-author of over twenty books, is the W. Guy McKenzie Professor of English at Florida State University. Recipient of five Florida State Teaching Awards, he has had work appear in the *Best American Poetry* and the *Pushcart Prize* series. Here, Kirby discusses Strand's discomfort with the ideal state and the way in which it ultimately helps to prefigure his work in *The Monument*.]

Strand's speakers' desire for self-effacement reaches a peak of seriousness in *The Story of Our Lives*, and that seriousness is announced by a change in style. In the words of the dust jacket, the poems collected here are "longer [in fact, there are only seven of them], more mysterious, more engrossing" than Strand's earlier work. One might add "more strenuous" to that list of adjectives; the reader of these poems really gets a sense of Jacob wrestling with the angel. The title work, for example, is in seven parts and deals almost claustrophobically with two people struggling both to live their lives and to read about them in a putative book that already seems to have been completed.

For example, in part 1 of "The Story of Our Lives" it is observed that "we sit beside each other on the couch, / reading about the couch," and not only do "we say it is ideal" but in fact "it is ideal" in the book the couple is reading. The ideal state is not necessarily a comfortable one in Strand's poetry, though; it is perhaps too substantive in a world in which the material is downplayed. As in earlier work, the atmosphere of the poem is soundless, almost motionless (except for the turning of the pages), and progressively darker. The room in which the action takes place is almost a world unto itself, and indeed "it is almost as if the room were the world" (97). The word *room* will have greater significance in other poems in this collection, but for the moment it is enough to say that it delimits the action by providing a barrier between the couple and a noisy world outside and also, on the strength of its soothing quietness, encourages the couple to keep their own egos in check.

In part 2 of "The Story of Our Lives," the man tries to push past the ideal state not only by living his life and reading about it but also by writing:

> I lean back and begin to write about the book.
> I write that I wish to move beyond the book,
> beyond my life into another life.

This makes sense: it turns out that the book the couple is reading is a bad book because it looks too far ahead and tells too much. For example, it says that the woman will fall in love with the man across the street and that the speaker will grow old without her. Glimmerings of Strand's early theme of the divided self are present here. When the speaker says, "The book describes much more than it should. / It wants to divide us," the reader knows not only that the couple may be separated but also that their individual selves are in danger (98).

These feelings turn out to be prophetic. Part 3 has the speaker rereading the "mysterious parts" of the book, especially the early ones that leave him feeling as though he's "dreaming of childhood." Having lost his focus on the here and now, the speaker feels (and reads that he's feeling) a sensation similar to that described in "Sleeping with One Eye Open" for example, or in "The Accident" and "The Man in the Mirror" (*Reasons*). The book-within-the-poem says:

> *A bleak crown rested uneasily on his head.*
> *He was the brief ruler of inner and outer discord,*
> *anxious in his own kingdom.*

(99)

As he confirms the horrible news of his own anxiety, the speaker is waiting for the woman to awake. In part 4, she seems to him to be secure, protected rather than vulnerable, and he is "moved by a desire to offer myself / to the house of your sleep." (As an objectification of things solid and unchanging as opposed to things ephemeral and unreliable, *house* is used here as *room* will be used in several other poems.) The more he watches her and the less he reads, the more it seems as though there will be a breakthrough into a higher state of happy calm. If he knows this, of course, then so will the book; so that when the speaker confesses, "I was tired and wanted to give up," he also says, "the book seemed aware of this. / It hinted at changing the subject" (100).

And that is the problem: the couple are followed everywhere by the book, and they will never lose their self-consciousness as long as the book masters their lives. It is worse than a mirror, which merely reflects, as the images in the book preexist and cause anxiety by announcing limits that cannot be transcended.

Part 5 deals with the paradox of longing for perfection, which of course cannot exist, since the anxiety of longing prevents the attainment of any perfect state. We know from earlier Strand poems that the perfect state is immaterial, unselfconscious, transcendent, but how can that state be reflected in the book, which is material, self-conscious to the extreme, and imminently mundane? No wonder the speaker observes ruefully, "if there were a perfect moment in the book, / it would be the last" (101). If the story of their lives ends, then so will their lives, and no Strand speaker to date, regardless of the depth of his despair, has expressed an interest in so ultimate a solution.

Clearly, it is lives that are important, not stories of lives. The book is the story of the couple's lives, and that is what is wrong: in part 6 they read, *"it was words that created divisions in the first place, / that created loneliness."* The couple need to stop narrating—more precisely, they need to stop being narrated to—and start living. As it is, all they are doing is proving that consciousness is a terrible thing.

The escape that seemed possible for this unlucky pair in part 4 of "The Story of Our Lives" never takes place. Struggle as they may, they cannot get away from the Möbius strip of self-consciousness that seems an inescapable aspect of the modern condition:

> You are asking me if I am tired,
> if I want to keep reading.
> Yes, I am tired.
> Yes, I want to keep reading.
> I say yes to everything.

In the final part of the poem, the people end as simulacra of themselves, "*the copies, the tired phantoms / of something they had been before.*" The book has the last word about the people and about itself: "*They are the book and they are nothing else*" (102–3).

Thomas Jefferson described himself as having a canine appetite for reading; here is a poem that turns that eighteenth-century notion on its head and has a book eating people. Perhaps this is the revenge of the written word: a Strand speaker was able to devour some poems in "Eating Poetry" (*Reasons*), but an entire book is too much for this couple to fend off, no matter how strenuously they resist. From librarians to advertisers, everyone offers us books as an unqualified good. But this poem seems to be saying that the wrong book can be, not merely deadly boring, but deadly.

If it is so dangerous for us to *tell* ourselves our own stories, perhaps a more healthful activity is suggested in the title of a poem called "The Untelling." Indeed, if "The Story of Our Lives" is an account of a long, losing battle against fatal self-consciousness, "The Untelling" is an account of an equally long but successful struggle. First, though, it will be helpful to look at three shorter poems that provide some vocabulary important to a reading of "The Untelling."

—David Kirby. "And Then I Thought of The Monument." *Mark Strand and the Poet's Place in Contemporary Culture.* (Columbia and London: University of Missouri Press. 1990): pp. 28–31.

Sven Birkerts on the Lack of Telos in Strand's Poetry

[Sven Birkerts is the director of students and core faculty writing instructor in Bennington College's MFA Program and an instructor in Emerson College's MFA Program. He is a prolific and respected critic/reviewer and the author of *The Gutenberg Elegies*. He received a National Book Critics Circle Citation for Excellence in Reviewing, among other awards. In this review, he discusses the lack of a telos and the tension that absence creates within the collection.]

...[W]e also find the long tour-de-force narratives "The Story of Our Lives" and "The Untelling," both of which pit narration against itself, showing how the memory tape can be played backward, undoing the causal chain until, as Eliot wrote, "What might have been and what has been / Point to one end, which is always present." In Strand's version, the real and the possible commingle in the perpetual present of art. He ends "The Untelling," a sequence in which the speaker is a writer wrestling with what might be either a memory or an imagined event, by putting the tail inside the snake's mouth; the writer begins the poem that we have, presumably, been reading. We read:

>He turned and walked to the house.
>He went to the room
>that looked out on the lawn.
>He sat and began to write:
>   THE UNTELLING
>   *To the Woman in the Yellow Dress*

While the conceit of these longer poems is interesting, the line-by-line progress is often tedious, without much to savor in the poetry itself.

—Sven Birkerts. "The Art of Absence" *The New Republic* 3, 961 (December 17, 1990): pp. 37.

CRITICAL ANALYSIS OF
"The Way It Is"

Wallace Stevens epigraph "The world is ugly. / And the people are sad." perfectly begins the very dark view of Strand's fear ravaged speaker. In this poem, suburbia becomes a nightmarish hell where neighbors act as birds of prey and the potential for violence sleeps one house over. Strand chose the poem to end his third book of poems. With its longer narrative structure and broadened concern with the public domain, it marks a change in Strand from the self-referential to the socially aware. The nightmare is no longer solely in the poet's head. It has come to the neighborhood to roost.

The title suggests a proclamation—a definitive fact that will clearly define life for the reader. The definition disheartens. The poem begins with the speaker spending a sleepless night. In stark contrast to the speaker, the things around him are "cold unruffled" as he stews through the evening. Immediately, despite the neatness of the couplets that end the first stanza, we know that something is awry. In the next apartment, the speaker's neighbor becomes a menace. Strand keeps the words and the image militaristic and threatening:

> My neighbor marches in his room,
> wearing the sleek
> mask of a hawk with a large beak.
> He stands by the window. A violet plume
>
> rises from his helmet's dome.

The neighbor marches, dons a helmet, and wears a mask of a hawk—symbols of ferocity, war and hunting. In the light of the open window, the neighbor is bathed in a white light from the moon, and his plume is violet, a traditional color of power. This threat lives next door to the speaker, creating an atmosphere of continual pending warfare.

That sense of danger is strangely intensified in the next stanza.

The neighbor sits in the park with his helmet, ready to go into battle, to begin his hunt. In his hand, he waves a little American flag as if to suggest that his aggression is for country, is the way of the country, a national pastime of warmongering, perpetual suburban defense. The neighbor is stealthy, according to the speaker, who cannot contain his fear. At any moment, the speaker expects violence to be enacted upon him. To protect himself, the speaker sinks into denial, pretending to be a dog under the table, convincing himself that were he a dog, and not a human, he would not be killed. In his America, people are killed before animals, focusing on the perversion of values in America.

As the speaker rests, delusional beneath the table, his neighbor's wife comes home. She controls her husband through sex. All descriptions of her are dark, suggesting some sort of complicity, "She seems to wade / through long flat rivers of shade. / The soles of her feet are black. / She kisses her husband's neck / and puts her hand inside his pants. //" She too may be as predatory as her husband, but her conquest is not death, it is sexual submission. The speaker seems to fear her as well. After the woman's sexual invitation, the couple has sexual relations, and she becomes the devil, the act, evil. He describes it "They roll on the floor, his tongue / is in her ear, his lungs reek with the swill and weather of hell."

But the evil is happening not only within the apartment building. It surrounds the speaker on every side. The scene on the streets is apocalyptic, harkening back to the Four Horsemen of the Apocalypse and images of the Holocaust. People lie on their backs in the street, weeping as ash settles around them. "Their clothes are torn from their backs. Their faces are worn. / Horsemen are riding around them, telling them why / they should die." The scene is unutterable despair, articulated simply, with the sort of psychic distance reminiscent of dreams.

In the next stanza, Strand returns to his speaker, who is still tossing restlessly in his imperturbable bed. The wife tells him that her husband is dead. The ambiguity here is devastating. Perhaps the wife killed the husband. Perhaps she did it for the speaker. Perhaps she is the carrier of the strange, "sleek" bird mask. As to whether she is more or less evil, we never know. The speaker accepts all the possibilities with little interest, glad only that the immediate threat is gone. He prays she is telling the truth, that he may be released from his paralyzing fear and insomnia. Around him the room is gray from the light of the moon and he drifts into a restless sleep with strange, portentous dreams.

As the speaker sleeps, he dreams that he is floating, then falling and incapable of calling for help. Even his scream is "vague." The speaker cannot even collect himself for that. In the next dream, he envisions himself in a park, "on horseback, surrounded by dark, / leading the armies of peace." This dream speaks to Robert Lowell's poem, "For the Union Dead." Union Colonel Robert Gould Shaw of the 54th Massachusetts Volunteer Regiment lead the first black regiment gathered in the North into battle, and as Lowell imagines it "…He rejoices in man's lovely, / peculiar power to choose life and die— / when he leads his black soldiers to death, / he cannot bend his back." When he died with his men in battle, Southern officers ordered his body to be thrown into a ditch with his men, and never marked to show how disgraceful they thought his actions. In Strand's poem, though the speaker tries to lead the armies of peace, his horse's legs will not bend; this horse and this man are monuments that represent little in actual lives. The horse is merely a facsimile of a horse as the speaker's courage is merely a facsimile of Shaw's courage. Unlike Shaw, the speaker drops the reigns, defeated as if to suggest that heroes can no longer exist in this nightmarish America.

All around the speaker, the normal sounds of the night continue. "Taxis stall / in the fog, passengers fall / asleep. Gas pours // from a tri-colored stack." Strand breaks his lines to emphasize the action: falling, stalling, pouring. The negativity pervades the entire scene, as things seem to happen uncontrollably. To combat the helplessness, people tell themselves stories again and again, trying to recreate their lives into something acceptable that is lived and chosen. Thematically, the poem speaks strongly to the couple in "The Story of Our Lives," who lose even the ability to tell their own story. The population is soulless. According to the speaker, "Everyone who has sold himself wants to buy himself back." Again, the feeling here is resignation. Too much has happened for these people to return to the lives they once envisioned for themselves. They have been corrupted, and the corruption is marked by starkly desperate imagery: "The night / eats into their limbs / like a blight."

The final stanza reaches a peak of despair and Strand expresses it quietly. "Everything dims. / The future is not what it used to be. / The graves are ready. The dead / shall inherit the dead." As the world darkens, and it is uncertain as to why it is so dark, Strand does not try to account for causality specifically, he merely claims that "the future is not what it used to be." Instead, the future leaves the people within it to become deadened or predatory or terribly afraid. They are among the emotionally dead, the untouchables who would kill a human before a dog, who would circle people, tearing at them and telling them why they are not worthy of life, or even those that huddle in their rooms and dream of fighting this vague evil but are defeated by their own thoughts before they even begin the battle. Ultimately, the meek shall not inherit the earth. The picture is much bleaker—hell on earth, where the dead inherit the already emotionally dead.

CRITICAL VIEWS ON
"The Way It Is"

Richard Howard on the Poet's Movement from Interior Dreamscape to Public Place

[Richard Howard teaches in the Writing Division of the School of the Arts, Columbia University. He is the author of eleven books of poetry, a gifted translator and a respected essayist on contemporary poetry. In this essay, Howard examines Strand's shift from an interior, self reflective, mirror-like landscape to the dramatic broadening of perspective in "The Way It Is."]

Strand's work since *Reasons for Moving* widens his scope, even as it sharpens his focus; just as he had divided his body against itself in order to discover an identity, he now identifies the body politic with his own In order to recover a division; in a series of political prospects, "Our Death," "From a Litany," "General," and finest of all, "The Way It Is," the poet conjugates the nightmares of Fortress America with his own stunned mortality to produce an apocalypse of disordered devotion:

> *Everyone who has sold himself wants to buy himself back.*
> *Nothing is done. The night*
> *eats into their limbs*
> *like a blight.*
> *Everything dims.*
> *The future is not what it used to be.*
> *The graves are ready. The dead*
> *shall inherit the dead.*

But what gives these public accents of Strand's their apprehensive relevance is not just a shrewd selection of details ("My neighbor marches in his room, / wearing the sleek / mask of a hawk with a large beak ... His helmet in a shopping bag, / he sits in the park, waving a small American flag"), nor any cosy contrast of the poet's *intimeries* against a gaining outer darkness ("Slowly I dance out of the burning house of my head. / And who isn't borne again and again into heaven?"). Rather it is the sense that public and private degradation, outer and inner weather, tropic and glacial decors (Saint Thomas and Prince Edward Islands, in fact) are all versions and visions of what Coleridge called the One Life, and that the whole of nature and society are no more than the churning content of a single and limitless human body—the poet's own. Such a sense—and in Strand it occupies all the senses ("the flesh of clouds burns / in the long corridors of sunlight. / I have changed. No one's death surprises me")—enables the poet to include much more life in these later poems of his; to invoke the wars of filiation, marriage and paternity; to explore the ennui of mere survival:

> *Must we settle for a routine happiness?*
> *Tell me something rotten about yourself.*
> *Tell me you've been to the doctor and he says*
> *I am going to die. Save me!*

and to endure the depredations of the past, the claims of merely *having been*:

> *Time tells me what I am. I change and am the same.*
> *I empty myself of my life and my life remains.*

—Richard Howard. "Mark Strand: 'The Mirror Was Nothing Without You.'" *Alone with America: Essays on the Art of Poetry in the United States Since 1950, Enlarged Edition* (New York, Atheneum: 1980): pp. 596–597.

HAROLD BLOOM ON THE POEM AS REPRESENTATIVE OF A SHIFT IN STRAND'S POETICS

[Harold Bloom is the Sterling Professor of Humanities at Yale University. He is a prolific and influential critic and the author of the renowned *Anxiety of Influence* and *The Western Canon*. In this essay, Bloom engages Strand's shift from his peripheral private phantasmagoria to a public phantasmagoria.]

Strand's unique achievement is to raise this mode to an aesthetic dignity that astonishes me, for I would not have believed, before reading him, that it could be made to touch upon a sublimity. *Darker* moves upon the heights in its final poems, "Not Dying" and the longer "The Way It Is," the first work in which Strand ventures out from his eye's first circle, toward a larger art. "Not Dying" opens in narcist desperation, and reaches no resolution, but its passion for survival is prodigiously convincing. "I am driven by innocence," the poet protests, even as like a Beckett creature he crawls from bed to chair and back again, until he finds the obduracy to proclaim a grotesque version of natural supernaturalism:

> I shall not die.
> The grave result
> and token of birth, my body
> remembers and holds fast.

"The Way It Is" takes its tone from Stevens at his darkest ("The world is ugly / And the people are sad") and quietly edges out a private phantasmagoria until this merges with the public phantasmagoria we all of us now inhabit. The consequence is a poem more surprising and profound than Lowell's justly celebrated "For the Union Dead," a juxtaposition made unavoidable by Strand's audacity in appropriating the same visionary area:

> I see myself in the park
> on horseback, surrounded by dark,
> leading the armies of peace.
> The iron legs of the horse do not bend.
>
> I drop the reins. Where will the turmoil end?
> Fleets of taxis stall in the fog, passengers fall
> asleep. Gas pours
>
> from a tri-colored stack.
> Locking their doors,
> people from offices huddle together,
> telling the same story over and over.

>Everyone who has sold himself wants to buy himself back.
>Nothing is done. The night
>eats into their limbs
>like a blight.
>
>Everything dims.
>The future is not what it used to be.
>The graves are ready. The dead
>shall inherit the dead.

Self-trained to a private universe of irreality, where he has learned the gnomic wisdom of the deep tautology, Strand peers out into the anxieties of the public world, to show again what can be shown, the shallow tautologies of a universal hysteria, as much a hysteria of protest as of societal repression. Wherever his poetry will go after *Darker*, we can be confident it goes as a perfected instrument, able to render an image not of any created thing whatsoever, but of every nightmare we live these days, separately or together.

>—Harold Bloom. "Dark and Radiant Peripheries: Mark Strand and A. R. Ammons," *Southern Review* (Winter 1972): pp. 133–41.

Peter Stitt on the Poem as an Attempt to Define the World

> [Peter Stitt is the Editor of *The Gettysburg Review* and a full Professor of English at Gettysburg College. He is a prolific reviewer and the author of *Uncertainty and Plenitude: Five Contemporary Poets* and *The World's Hieroglyphic Beauty: Five American Poets*. In this review, he examines the alienation of early Strand speakers based on their perceptions of reality.]

A partial explanation for this intense sense of alienation may be found in how this early speaker characterizes reality. It is perhaps his paranoia that makes him emphasize so strongly the dangers that lurk there. Injury and illness are among these but most important is the fact of death, the ultimate assault of nature against the self. The poem "Violent Storm" expresses much of this feeling by talking about the dangers inherent in bad weather. Superficial people may be able to party as the hurricane bears down upon the coast, it is true,

> But for us, the wide-awake, who tend
> To believe the worst is always waiting
> Around the next corner or hiding in the dry,
> Unsteady branch of a sick tree, debating
> Whether or not to fell the passerby,
> It has a sinister air.

This central consciousness is also fastidious, apparently finding much of the real world ugly—certainly much uglier than the "bright landscapes" he concocts in his own head. The poem "The Way It Is" is an attempt to define the general appearance and nature of the world, with its epigraph taken from Stevens ("The world is ugly. / And the people are sad.") and its direct concluding stanza: "Everything dims. / The future is not what it used to be. / The graves are ready. The dead / shall inherit the dead."

So deeply does the speaker feel the ugliness of reality, its power to render death and destruction upon him, that he attempts to retreat farther and farther from it. Through his death-consciousness, he diminishes the world until it virtually disappears into nothingness: "I grow into my death. / My life is small / and getting smaller. The world is green. / Nothing is all." Another poem expresses the same desire paradoxically: "More is less. / I long for more." The closer reality draws to nothingness, the greater looms the power of the mind and the world it creates for itself. This movement gives rise to two of the most important issues in Strand's early poetry—the question of identity and the question of knowledge. How is man to be defined if he is this radically alien to nature? And what can such a man know of a world so foreign to him?

—Peter Stitt. "Stages of Reality: The Mind/Body Problem in Contemporary Poetry" *The Georgia Review* 37: 1 (Spring 1983): pp. 202.

CRITICAL ANALYSIS OF
"Elegy for My Father"

"Elegy for My Father" is one of Strand's most striking poems, for the power of its litany, for the presence of the usually distant poet, and for its foreshadowing of later poems, like *Dark Harbor*. Strand places readers immediately into his psyche by providing the dates of his father's life. This notion clearly states that unlike other poems, this speaker will be Mark Strand, a son trying to reconcile the loss of his father and by extension, a part of himself.

The first of the poem's six sections is entitled "The Empty Body," suggesting a certain level of psychic distance brought about presumably from the shock of seeing his father's dead body. Throughout the section, Strand sets up the dichotomy of all that is in the world and in the room, the father's hands, his arms, his mouth, "the distant sun," "the pale green light of winter"; all were there save his father. He repeats the line over and over "you were not there," it becomes a litany of grief, a way in which the living son tries to accept his new reality by stating and re-stating what he sees to be true but can hardly believe. By calling to the father in the second person, there is still the suggestion of a connection, as if the reader believes he can still speak with the dead and find some sort of closure in that way.

In an attempt to gather the answers he feels he needs as a son, the poet directs questions to his father, questions that are at first flippant, then serious. The first answers suggest what one might tell a child, as the poet asks questions of his father with the same sort of vulnerability a child might show. "What did you wear? / *I wore a blue suit, a white shirt, yellow tie, and yellow socks.* / What did you wear? / *I wore nothing. A scarf of pain kept me warm.*" In this way, the son tries to collect answers to questions that are so emotional and clouded by memory that they are hard to articulate. By the end of the section, the father becomes so exhausted he can no longer answer the questions; he can only repeat them back in affirmation to his son. The section gains much of its power because it is so reminiscent of Strand himself. The father's answers which initially joke also ultimately lead to a larger truth, one in which the son has absolute faith. They suggest a gnosis for Strand's central themes and poetic discourse.

The third section, "Your Dying," is the longest and most agonized, appropriately so to mirror the struggle of the family waiting for the father's body to yield to what his spirit had already accepted. Throughout this section, the poet blames his father for his seeming determination to die. He begins the section "Nothing could stop you. / Not the best day. Not the quiet. Not the ocean rocking. / You went on with your dying." Strand creates a litany, naming meticulously all the things that formerly brought joy but could no longer touch the father. The pace picks up, moved by short phrases and parallel constructions. The effect is accusatory and furious. Strand repeats the claim that neither the father's son (Strand himself) nor his daughter could stop him, and the betrayal and hurt evident in the statement is devastating, particularly as the poet tries by referring himself in the third person, as the son, to distance himself from the pain. That struggle provides tension, giving the section a breathless feeling. In the end of the section, nothing can bring the father back, "Not your breathing. Not your life. / Not the life you wanted. / Not the life you had. / Nothing could stop you." The last lines show that neither memory nor hope has hold of the father now; he is irretrievable and the son cannot yet reconcile the loss.

By the fourth section, "Your Shadow," the shadow is all that remains of the father. It becomes the inheritance of the son who chronicles its movement through the past. It travels from "The Newsboys Home," "The streets of New York," "the street of Montreal," "Mexico City where you wanted to leave it." The son effortlessly relates the details of his father's past, showing his investment in the details. In some way, they have been his formative details as well; in following the path of his father's life, even metaphorically, the poet becomes even more intimately acquainted with the reality of his father's dying and what that loss truly is, from memory to corporeal reality. The poet/son retraces his father's steps, gathering his father's past. He uses the metaphor of reclaiming the lost shadow from all the places it had been with the father. After the elder Strand died, the shadow was left behind to mourn his death. Strand imagines it sleeping "at the mouth of the furnace" waiting for the father and eating "ashes for bread." It eventually finds its way to Strand's home when it cannot find the father. It settles around the son, as if finding a second home. For Strand, it is not enough to be second hand, to be somehow the same as his father and yet other. He chooses instead to send the shadow away. "Your shadow is yours. I told it so. I said it was yours. / I have carried it with me too long. I give it back." In this final act, the son is emancipated from the father, living on his on terms after being haunted by the father and the father's past. It frees him to grieve and move on.

With this new understanding, Strand finds himself watching the other mourners with a certain impersonal distance. The fury has subsided a little, and now Strand is ready to relate the immediate scene, moving from his own mourning to that of those around him. Their mourning borders on hysteria. They mourn him by recreating him, in memory, in his last set of clothes, in the money that will get him into heaven or out of hell, with the prayers they send forth, with the begging they do at his bedside. There is no way to reach the dying man.

> But they cannot drag the buried light from your veins.
> They cannot reach your dreams.
> Old man, there is no way.
> Rise and keep rising, it does no good.
> They mourn for you the way they can.

Despite all of the machinations of the mourners, the pleas, the hand wringing, the deals with God, the dead man is gone. Strand has already released him in a way that the others cannot.

In the sixth section, the New Year has come and with it, both the metaphors of death and rebirth that already pervade the poem. The imagery of this section only serves to reinforce that notion. In this winter scape, the poet tells his father, "Nobody knows you." The father is truly gone. He lies under "the weather of stones," acted upon and inanimate. It is a place without escape, totally irrevocable, a realization that the poet has been coming to throughout the poem. His father's friends lie in their beds, pleasantly enjoying sleep, its physical reality, and think nothing of the dead man. The father sees nothing now; this lack of sight and the knowledge it brings is one more form of death. The poet repeats his opening line, as if to confirm once more that "It is over. It is the winter and the new year." The repetition suggests a new setting, a new time, a new mindset. It is a walking away from the past and the power of the father's memory. The poet acknowledges finally "And nothing comes back. / Because it is over. / Because there is silence instead of a name. / Because it is winter and the new year." The litany becomes all the reasons that Strand is moving on, and provide all of the apology necessary for invoking the dead again. The litany creates a cycle that mirrors that of death and rebirth, powerfully reinforcing the themes carved out over the course of six sections.

CRITICAL VIEWS ON
"Elegy for My Father"

LAURENCE LIEBERMAN ON THE USE OF LITANY

[Laurence Lieberman is the author of twelve volumes of poetry and three books of critical essays. He is on the faculty in the University of Illinois MFA program and has been the poetry editor at the University of Illinois Press since 1971. In this essay, Lieberman asserts that the use of litany creates a dirge that heightens the profundity of the mourning in the poem.]

In "Elegy for My Father," the stately, slow-paced, hypnotic dirge that begins the new volume, Strand amplifies the serial mode of litany. Exhibiting a remarkable range of technical virtuosity, he adapts the device of image chains to six widely varying fantasias. In each, a simple statement—flat and blunt—is repeated at irregular intervals, and operates less like a conventional refrain than an aria or leitmotiv in an opera. The statement tends to fade, to become hidden, vanishing into a chanted monotony, but it subtly builds resonance in the reader's ear and accumulates a force of quiet, but irreversible, authority. "Nothing could stop you. You went on with your dying."

In "Your Dying," the midsection of the poem, the father's unswerving complicity in his progress toward death exalts the process of welcoming death into an austere discipline, an artistry that by its propulsive force of negation, by its revulsion from nature and human society, sends all things into orbit around itself. He achieves an absolute solipsism of dying, which is mirrored by the son's solipsism of mourning. The total psychic withdrawal from life, paradoxically, adds a dimension to being alive, a deepening and heightening of spirit, which threatens the comfortable world of the living, the friends and neighbors who "doze in the dark / of pleasure and cannot remember." The living are shocked into a panic of opposition—they are wavery, unstable, flighty, aimless. The act of dying easily imposes its higher will and design on the chaos of life, its deathly order on the disorder that is prevalent everywhere.

The whole book is a profound act of mourning; hence, the aptly grotesque irony of the fifth section of the elegy, titled "Mourning," a Kafkaesque caricature of conventional funerals in which the mourning process, so indispensable to healing the psychic wounds of bereavement, is debased and betrayed by self-pity. The common blind refusal to accept death is parodied as a procession of beggarly kin pleading with the corpse to come back to life, perverting the funeral rites into a litany of gamy ruses to pamper and coddle him into not dying, as if a complex gymnastics of undying could undo the death:

> They mourn for you.
> When you rise at midnight ...
> They sit you down and teach you to breathe.
> And your breath burns,
> It burns the pine box and the ashes fall like sunlight.
> They give you a book and tell you to read.
> They listen and their eyes fill with tears.
> The women stroke your fingers.
> They comb the yellow back into your hair.
> They shave the frost from your beard.
> They knead your thighs.
> They dress you in fine clothes.
> They rub your hands to keep them warm.
> They feed you. They offer you money.
> They get on their knees and beg you not to die.
> When you rise at midnight they mourn for you.
> They close their eyes and whisper your name over and over.
> But they cannot drag the buried light from your veins.
> They cannot reach your dreams.

So far from resisting, or denying, the reality of his father's death, Strand's own mode of mourning is to follow his father into dying, taking as many steps down the path toward death as possible short of dying himself, and though this process culminates in a valiant entreaty invoking the invisible powers for release from the bondage to his father's corpse ("It came to my house. / It sat on my shoulders. / Your shadow is yours. I told it so. I said it was yours. / I have carried it with me too long. I give it back."), it is clear from the other poems of the present volume that the elegy is only the first milestone in an interior odyssey in which he follows a long, intricate course in developing a new poetics that recapitulates his vision of his father's dying. Strand is obsessed, in poem after poem, with absence, vanishings, disappearance of parts of his own psyche. The opening litany of the elegy, "The Empty Body," suggests that the author's obsession with disappearance grew initially out of the shock of witnessing his father's dead body. He could not fathom or accept the emptiness—the spiritual evacuation—of the corpse:

> The hands were yours, the arms were yours,
> But you were not there.
> The eyes were yours, but they were closed and would not open....
> The body was yours, but you were not there.
> The air shivered against its skin.
> The dark leaned into its eyes.
> But you were not there.

>   —Laurence Lieberman. "Mark Strand: The Book of Mourning."
> *Beyond the Muse of Memory: Essays on Contemporary American Poets*
> (Columbia and London, University of Missouri Press: 1995): pp.
> 220–222. Originally appeared in *The Yale Review*, 1968.

RICHARD HOWARD ON THE POEM AS AN AFFIRMATION OF LIFE

> [Richard Howard teaches in the Writing Division of the School of the Arts, Columbia University. He is the author of eleven books of poetry, a gifted translator and a respected essayist on contemporary poetry. In this essay, Howard examines the way in which Strand's insistent refusal of his father's shadow, coupled with the insistence of the poetic structure, ultimately affirms process rather than stagnation.]

One more celebration of an empty place, this elegy is an emblematic trajectory, a six-poem acknowledgment of the necessity to put off knowledge, to deny, to refuse, to gainsay: "There were no secrets. There was nothing to say." Strand insists, or broods, which is his brand of insistence, on the importance, for individual survival ("they cannot reach your dreams"), of rejecting that extremity of consciousness which process, which historical existence, cannot endure or transcend. Sometimes—later on in the book—he is wistful about such ecstatic apprehensions ("If only there were a perfect moment ... if only we could live in that moment"), but he is quite certain that they are not available to him, that they are not within life, as indeed the sense of the word *ecstasy* makes evident they are not. So Strand divides to conquer, divides the self to conquer the self ("you are the neighbor of nothing"), for the price of experience, experience which Blake has told us cannot be bought for a song, is negation.

Which is why Strand writes his lament not in verse but in the very dialect of negation, in prose, the one linguistic medium out to eliminate itself, to use itself up in the irrecoverable rhythms of speech rather than in the angelic (or ecstatic) measures of repetition and return. No recurrence, no refrain here, but the horror of knowing too much, of suffering more than is to be borne: "I have carried it with me too long, I give it back," Strand says to his father's "shadow", that Blakean spector of the mortal body which is life without time, or death within eternity where "there is silence instead of a name." For once we accept, once we put on the consciousness of others, Strand implies, we are lost. Such an assumption is a "rejoicing among ruins," a "crystal among the tombs"; to say No to consciousness—

> ... to stand in a space is to
> forget time, to forget time
> is to forget death ...

is the one way of evincing and yet evading the horror: negation is a mask which points to itself (as a mask), advancing. The prose sentences of "Elegy for My Father" are for life in their refusal to recuperate a rhythm, to reverse. They insist upon process, upon the rudiments of narrative ("The beginning is about to occur. The end is in sight") which will get past those nodal points when it all becomes so saturated with Being that life has nowhere to go and so cannot go on. Strand's poem is a way of outdistancing the mind in its submission to consciousness—it is a discarding in order to pick up the blank card, the next ... "that silence is the extra page."

> —Richard Howard. "Mark Strand: 'The Mirror Was Nothing Without You.'" *Alone with America: Essays on the Art of Poetry in the United States Since 1950, Enlarged Edition* (New York, Atheneum: 1980): pp. 599–600. Originally appeared in the *Ohio Review* (1974).

DAVID KIRBY ON THE POEM AS LOSS OF SELF

> [David Kirby, author or co-author of twenty-one books, is the W. Guy McKenzie Professor of English at Florida State University. Recipient of five Florida State Teaching Awards, he has had work appear in the *Best American Poetry* and the *Pushcart Prize* series. In this essay, he posits the poem as a loss of self and the development of a poetic voice that would ultimately result in *The Monument*.]

Perhaps none of this would have been possible, though, had Strand not written "Elegy for My Father (Robert Strand 1908–68)." This magnificent poem, one of the great elegies of the English language, distinguishes itself from *Lycidas* and *Adonais* and *In Memoriam* by being more a poem of dispersal than they are, a poem of cleaning up and giving away. The loss of a father is in part a loss of self for any man, provided he is able to lose it. However, as one might expect from Strand at this point, to lose that self takes effort.

"Elegy for My Father" consists of six parts. Part 1, "The Empty Body," is a fairly straightforward anatomy of the body's physical aspects in contrast to its departed spirit. "The hands were yours, the arms were yours," begins the poem, "But you were not there." There is no pain anymore, no secrets. The world encroaches, but it can no longer trouble the dead man:

> The body was yours, but you were not there.
> The air shivered against its skin.
> The dark leaned into its eyes.
> But you were not there.
> (85)

Part 2, "Answers," is a dialogue in which each question (except the last two) is asked twice and receives two answers, the first literal and the second figurative; the first response is always true, the second truer. For example, when the son asks the father whom he slept with, the father says a different woman every night, but when the question is repeated, the father says he always slept alone—each of us sleeps this way, and none more so than the libertine. In this section the father seems at first a cynic ("*nothing means much to me anymore*"), then a skeptic ("*I don't know, I have never known*" [86]), and ultimately a stoic. Amid the multiplicity of answers, the section concludes with an unambiguous acknowledgment of death's finality: when the son asks how long he should wait for the father, the answer is that he should not wait, that the father is tired and wants to lie down. "Are you tired and do you want to lie down?" asks the son (86). But the father is so exhausted by this point that he can only repeat the question.

Silent now, the father begins the last stage of his dying. The third part of the poem, "Dying," is the longest, for death is never easy. The father seems determined; the section begins, "Nothing could stop you," and the line is repeated throughout. In elaboration of that statement, most of the other lines begin with the word *not*: "Not your friends who gave you advice. / Not your son. Not your daughter who watched you grow small." Grief spills like water here as the father himself wakes at night, wet with tears, as the "son who thought you would live forever" observes over and over, now in anguish, now numbly, "You went on with your dying" (86–87).

The father's effort over, the speaker must now make his own. The father achieves a kind of completion in death; the divided self that troubles so many others in Strand's poetry comes together here in part 4, entitled "The Shadow." Still, the surviving son must assist the departed father, just as the living pray for or attend the dead in formally organized religions. Here, the speaker catalogs each appearance of the father's shadow and the shadow's return to its source:

> The rooms in Belém where lizards would snap at mosquitos have given it back.
> The dark streets of Manaus and the damp streets of Rio have given it back.
> Mexico City where you wanted to leave it has given it back.
> (88)

The most important place for the shadow to have lingered is in the speaker's own house, where "it sat on my shoulders." But the speaker must be his own man now. This section ends with the speaker's angry address, not to the father whom he loved, but to the father's shadowy partial self, the abstraction the dead become when the living reduce them to terms that are manageable and false:

> Your shadow is yours. I told it so. I said it was yours.
> I have carried it with me too long. I give it back.
> (89)

As in "The Untelling," one succeeds here by failing: to never write the poem is to write the best poem ever, and to reject a limited version of a dead father is to have that father always in his fullness. The two works also have in common the fact that the speaker in each, while on the surface honoring something exterior (a poem, a father), is secretly engaged in his own salvation.

Among other things, "Elegy for My Father" is a poem noticeable for its symmetry. The first two comparatively brief sections introduce the father in body and spirit, the longer third and fourth sections deal with the father's hard-fought dying and the son's equally difficult struggle to both honor his father and live his own life, and the two short, final sections describe the public mourning for the father and the son's private consolation.

52

In part 5, "Mourning," those who knew the dead man simply "mourn for you the way they can" (90). However, in the poem's last part, "The New Year," there is genuine closure as the speaker moves beyond the clichés of traditional mourning to make peace on his own terms with the spirit of the departed parent, now "the neighbor nothing."

> —David Kirby. "And Then I Thought of *The Monument.*" *Mark Strand and the Poet's Place in Contemporary Culture* (Columbia and London, University of Missouri Press: 1990): pp. 38–41.

SVEN BIRKERTS ON THE POEM'S INFLUENCES

> [Sven Birkerts is the director of students and core faculty writing instructor at Bennington College's MFA Program and an instructor in Emerson College's MFA Program. He is a prolific and respected critic/reviewer and the author of *The Gutenberg Elegies*. He received a National Book Critics Circle Citation for Excellence in Reviewing among other awards. In this review, he discusses Strand's treatment of absence through borrowed style elements, taken from Spanish and South American writers.]

For Strand, it is thus: we have been hurled into being and there is no immanent or transcendent ground for the self. Yet we possess, in uneasy wakefulness, a capacity to perceive and to reflect. This is our curse, for it cuts us off from the serene unknowingness of the rest of the natural world. The traditional recourse has been religion—to believe that we are not held simply within ourselves, but, in some fashion, within the love (or purpose) of a higher being. But there is no hint of this in Strand, not anywhere. He has rigorously pruned from his lines anything that could suggest a telos, or a redemption of pain and isolation. His figures are at large in space; they move about in time—time afflicts them—but they never progress *to* anything. (...)

With the publication in 1973 of *The Story of Our Lives*, Strand made what was for him a significant departure, leaving behind the short poems, so distinctive in their polished austerity, to explore the rhetorical and narrative possibilities of the long poem. The book opens with the powerful "Elegy for My Father," a poem in six sections. Strand's lines are loose, often repetitive, but they press at their subject with a mounting urgency. In the absence of any argument or metaphysics, the sheer perseverance of address is impressive. Strand succeeds by varying the pitch and approach, moving from the affectless pronouncements of the first section:

> The hands were yours, the arms were yours,
> But you were not there.
> The eyes were yours, but they were closed
>   and would not open.

to a more urgent reimagining of the process of dying in section three:

> You put your watch to your ear.
> You felt yourself slipping.
> You lay on the bed.
> You folded your arms over your chest and
>   you dreamed of the world without you.

to the final section, which achieves an impersonal, even elemental perspective, integrating the loss into the rhythm of seasonal passage:

> It is winter and the new year.
> Nobody knows you.
> Away from the stars, from the rain of light,
> You lie under the weather of stones.

The elegy manifests rather overtly the influences of Spanish and South American poets. Strand freely adopts the surreal particularizations favored by Neruda and Vallejo ("The years, the hours, that would not find you / Turned in the wrists of other.") and the recursive repetitions of Carlos Drummond de Andrade, whom Strand has translated.

—Sven Birkerts. "The Art of Absence." *The New Republic* 3, 961 (December 17, 1990): pp. 37.

Edward Byrne on the Poem as a Precursor to *A Blizzard of One*

[Edward Byrne is a Professor of American Literature and creative writing at Valparaiso University. He is the author of five volumes of poetry and the editor of *Valparaiso Poetry Review*. In this essay, he considers the poem as part of the poetic evolution that resulted in Strand's Pulitzer Prizing winning volume as well as his later book of essays, *The Weather of Words*.]

The same concerns voiced in *Blizzard of One* were evident more than a decade ago when readers encountered *The Continuous Life* (1990): "When the weight of the past leans against nothing, and the sky / Is no more than remembered light, and the stories of cirrus / And cumulus come to a close, and all the birds are suspended in flight, / Not every man knows what is waiting for him ..." ("The End"). Although death as "the central concern" and the issue of scenes in a poet's life being witnessed "as they exist in passing" may be most clearly evident earlier in *The Story of Our Lives* (1973), especially "Elegy for My Father" and "The Untelling," those compelling poems in memory of his parents starting and concluding this important and influential volume that appeared more than a quarter century ago:

> It is winter and the new year.
> Nobody knows you.
> Away from the stars, from the rain of light,
> You lie under the weather of stones.
>   ["Elegy for My Father"]

> He leaned forward over the paper
> and he wrote:
>
> *... They moved beyond the claims*
> *of weather, beyond whatever news there was,*
> *and did not see the dark beginning to deepen*
> *in the trees and bushes, and rise in the folds*
> *of their own dresses and in the stiff white*
> *of their own shirts.*
>   ["The Untelling"]

Here, as well as elsewhere in many of his poems, particularly more recent works, Strand's attention to suspended moments or different measurements of time again recalls his earliest pleasure of reading McLeish's poem "both about time and in time." However, these poems also resemble Robert Penn Warren's repeated explorations of time, timelessness, and no-time, especially in his later poetry—or as Warren would state it in "There's a Grandfather's Clock in the Hall," those moments when "Time thrusts through the time of no-Time." Though perhaps not as strong as other influences, Warren's distinctive poetic figure is often present, lingering not far behind the lines of Strand's poetry, such as those in "The Garden" (*The Late Hour*, 1978), a poem dedicated to Warren, and one reminiscent of "The Untelling".

> —Edward Byrne. "Weather Watch: Mark Strand's *The Weather of Words*." Valparaiso Poetry Review: Contemporary Poetry and Poetics II: 2 (Spring/Summer 2001): www.valpo.edu/english/vprv2n2.html.

CRITICAL ANALYSIS OF
"Dark Harbor"

Despite its portentous title, "Dark Harbor" is a poem of redemption, an act of reclamation through song and through a direct confrontation with mortality. In typical Strand fashion, it is not enough to casually imagine an afterlife; instead, he actively constructs it, forcing both he and the reader to face a landscape that may well be death, where reality is made exclusively by the dead and for the dead. The living are too earnest in their every day pursuits, assuming consequences that simply don't exist in this new world where death is not the ultimate consequence.

Strand begins the book length poem with a short prologue, entitled, "Proem." In it, the narration is third person, presumably a poet, who chooses to leave behind his town and all that he knows. As he journeys: "he would move his arms // And begin to mark, almost as a painter would, / The passages of greater and lesser worth, the silken / Topes and calls to this or that, coarsely conceived…." The poet is being posited as painter, his search for detail and symbols a part of his work; and as he walks away, he finally finds himself able to breathe. In this uncharted landscape, he tells himself, "This is the life." In the first section, the point of view shifts so that the "he" of the first "proem" has become the "I" in the interior. The reader is to believe the narrator has entered "the night without end" a metaphor for death, the very thing that so many of Strand's earlier characters are trying to avoid. In this place, "it is best to be ready, for the ash / Of the body is worthless and only goes so far." In essence, Strand is freeing his narrator to take the journey without the encumbrance of the body and its sundry boundaries. With the mind, there are no such restrictions, and that is part of the journey foretold in "Proem."

In the second section, the speaker claims "I am writing from a place you have never been," calling readers to attention. This will not be death of hellfire and brimstone; it is somewhere else, regardless of punishment and godliness. What is here is an extension of the mind, a greater capacity for joy and emotion unclouded by obligation. When "the heavenly choir at the barbecue" is "adjusting its tone to serve the occasion," all the participants are "staring, stunned into magnitude." This place opens up the possibility of awe and celebration. He asserts in the third section that this is a pre-body place; people have been here before:

> And you pass by unsure if this coming back is a failure
> Or a sign of success, a sign that the time has come
> To embrace your origins as you would yourself,

It is the place primordial, both pre and post body. Here memory coincides, in the shape of Mom and Dad, in the shape of dreams, in the shape of the landscape. It is both familiar and exotic. In the fifth section, the speaker views the other side of the equation: the living, and claims:

> On the other side, no one is looking this way.
> They are committed to obstacles,
> To the textures and levels of darkness,
> To the tedious enactment of duration,
> And they labor not for bread or love
>
> But to perpetuate the balance between the past
> And the future. They are the future as it
> Extends itself, just as we are the past
>
> Coming to terms with itself.

In this stanza, the living are trying hard to provide for their families. They work with practical concerns to assure a future. The dead don't need to do that; their time goes on. Their notion of the past, as with writers who have the possibility of writing something immortal, is marked differently, less concerned with practicality. There existence is no longer finite. Strand suggests that the dead view the past to make sense of it. That is their project. As a poet, the narrator reconciles with memory, whether it be ancestral or a studied heritage, as in the case of the sections of *Dark Harbor* that pay homage to poets of Strand's past, Octavio Paz, Wallace Stevens, John Ashbery, Richard Howard, Rilke, and others.

In section X, Strand presents one of his most central trials as a poet and inheritor of the art:

> It is a dreadful cry that rises up,
> Hoping to be heard, that comes to you
> As you wake, so your day will be spent
>
> In the futile correction of a distant longing.

He relates the process of writing and re-writing, its ongoing frailties. In a sort of ars poetica, Strand attempts to answer why he writes, why he listens to the voices of misery, of heartbreak, of fear, and of pain:

> And you have no choice but to follow their prompting,
>
> Saving something of that sound, urging the harsh syllables
> Of disaster into music.

He continues a few lines later:

> How do you turn pain
> Into its own memorial, how do you write it down,
>
> Turning it into itself as witnessed
> Through pleasure, so it can be known, even loved,
> As it lives in what it could not be.

This, it seems is the project of the book, to conceive of how poetry can articulate that which could not be spoken, indeed, could barely be endured. It posits the music of poetry as something that might make pain something loved, something more than the events themselves. It might make immortality. Moving ahead to the sixteenth section, Strand invokes his acknowledged mentor, Wallace Stevens, "It is true, as someone has said, that in/ A world without heaven all is farewell." This is a frightening truth, to suggest that without a god figure, the end is truly the end. Loved ones will not be rediscovered in heaven. They are simply gone from our lives. The notion forces a different way of living. Strand continues to drive the point home throughout the poem, insisting that nothing will keep that truth from being, not ignorance, not lack of feeling, not denial. It is simultaneously what the poet must endure and must express. It is the human condition, and the condition of the songster that so saddens Orpheus, the poet's alter ego, in section XXVIII:

> Orpheus can change the world
> For a while, but he cannot save it, which is his despair.
> It is a brilliant limitation that he enacts and
>
> He knows it, which is why the current of his song
> Is always mournful, always sad. It is even worse
> For the rest of us.

The plight is the same. The poet can change the world for as long as the reader chooses to engage the song. In a sense, Strand is commenting on his own early works, which are so often described as "dark;" he offers a compelling reason for that darkness. Also, in this section, as in others, a mirror appears, but like the images that will follow in other sections, that mirror shows a paradise that cannot be touched.

> A shadowed glass held within its frozen calm an image
> Of abundance, a bloom of humanness, a hymn in which
> The shapes and sounds of Paradise are buried.

It is the trick of the mirror, to make visible that which cannot be accessed, like perfection and the act that might save the world. Still, the act of writing restores the spirit simply because it is an attempt to unearth the mirror image and the inaccessible or, impossible to articulate, human truth that is reflected. It is always the fulfillment of the mirror image for which the poet strives.

Along with Orpheus, Strand invokes another mythic name, Marsyas, the satyr, skinned by Apollo for daring to challenge the god to a contest of music. The poet ruminates on the plight of the satyr, whose blood became a river, whose song was beautiful and lost. He questions the use of the body:

> Or is a body scraped
>
> From the bone of experience, the chart of suffering
> To be read in such ways that all flesh might be redeemed,
> At least for the moment, the moment it passes into song.

Strand returns again to the notion that music is redemptive, that the body in service of music is made meaningful. He builds this understanding throughout the poem so that it culminates in the last section. In the dark harbor, this landscape that is the afterlife, or some form of immortality or perhaps, more accurately, post mortality, there is some form of faith, or power, and it is song, the word, poetry, and those who sing it are angels. In the final section, the speaker arrives in a misty place to find poets huddled around a fire:

> there were many poets who wished to be alive again.
> They were ready to say the words they had been unable to say—
>
> Words whose absence had been the silence of love,
> Of pain, and even of pleasure.

Finally, he figures these former poets as something more divine than a set of lost wishes and lost words:

> I looked away to the hills
> Above the river, where the golden lights of sunset
> And sunrise are one and the same, and saw something flying
> Back and forth, fluttering its wings. Then it stopped in mid-air.
> It was an angel, one of the good ones, about to sing.

This final angel is redemption not only for the dead poets, who thought themselves lost, but also for the world at large, who can listen to the song, and if they are careful not to look back, this Orphic angel might bring them back from the dead.

CRITICAL VIEWS ON
"Dark Harbor"

CHRISTOPHER BENFEY ON THE POEM AS A KIND OF
ARS POETICA

[Christopher Benfey is Professor of English at Mount Holyoke. He is the author of several critical studies, among them a biography of Stephen Crane which was named a "notable book of the year" by the New York Times and most recently, he published *Degas in New Orleans: Encounters in the Creole World of Kate Chopin and George Washington Cable*, which the *Chicago Tribune* named on the 1997's ten most important books. In this review, he shows how the influences and the techniques converge in *Dark Harbor*, to arrive at a kind of ars poetica.]

Strand has worked steadily on, transforming himself from a surrealistic, "deep-image" poet of the '60s (a description that I will qualify in a moment) to someone who, in a different voice, eludes easy categorization. His new book is a kind of summing up: of the poet's task in dark times; of a poet's engagement with predecessors and contemporaries; of what poetry can make, and make happen. *Dark Harbor* is a fine occasion for making sense of Strand. (...)

This is the voice of *Dark Harbor*, Strand's hauntingly beautiful new volume. It is a single long poem consisting of a "Proem" and forty-five numbered sections. The long poem in English derives from at least three traditions, each with its own conventions and generic expectations: the epic (*The Bridge*, *Paterson*, *The Waste Land*, among twentieth-century examples); the novel in verse (Vikram Seth's *The Golden Gate*); and the sonnet sequence (Lowell's *Notebook* and its spill-off volumes, *Berryman's Sonnets*). *Dark Harbor* belongs to the third category; its major forebears are Rilke's *Sonnets to Orpheus* and Stevens's longer poetic sequences. The elastic, three-line stanzas, with a good deal of enjambment across lines and across stanzas, also derive from Stevens, and from various versions of terza rima reaching back to Dante (a bit of whose work Strand has recently translated). (...)

Strand has always had what Stevens called "a mind of winter," more attuned to austerities than to luxuries. He is in love with negatives, privatives, the empty and erased. "I would like to be / In that solitude of soundless things, in the random / Company of the wind, to be weightless, nameless" (xviii). When he mulls over "the seasonal possibilities" in one poem (xvii) and vows in another to take as his muse "The burning / Will of weather" ("Proem"), it's winter, predictably, that he apostrophizes:

> O pretty densities of white on white!
> O snowflake lost in the vestibules of April
>   air!
>
> Beyond the sadness-the empty
>   restaurants,
> The empty streets, the small lamps shining
> Down on the town-I see only the stretches
>
> Of ice and snow, the straight pines, the
>   frigid moon.

In these late poems, Strand has begun to notice the snow in his own hair: "Here comes old age, dragging a tale of soft / Inconvenience, of golfing in Florida, / Of gumming bad food." He sees himself increasingly as an aging poet writing in dark times. In a poem that links him compellingly with Ashbery—it is not the only bow to Ashbery in this book—Strand notes that "There is / A current of resignation that charges even our most / Determined productions." In another poem, where Whitman is the honored companion ("Me at my foulest, the song of me ..."), Strand says flatly, his own Jeremiah, "These are bad times. Idiots have stolen the moonlight. / They cast their shadowy pomp wherever they wish."

Such poems, in which Strand acknowledges a community of poets, both quick and dead, to keep the practicing poet company, are among the most powerful in *Dark Harbor*. In poem xxvii, six unnamed poets are invoked and praised—the first three for achievements of rhetoric ("I love how the beautiful echoed / Within the languorous length of his sentences, / Forming a pleasing pointless commotion"), the second three for intensities of vision ("Of yet another the precision, the pursuit of rightness, / Balance, some ineffable decorum, the measured, circuitous / Stalking of the subject, turning surprise to revelation").

It is a guessing game. Is that Wallace Stevens behind Door No. 1? Elizabeth Bishop behind No. 4, or No. 6? But more important than any particular identification are the terms of appreciation here. Three poets who verge on absurdity and chaos, three poets who verge on revelation. What Strand admires is the pushing to extremes, the flirtation with the pointless (here meaning, also, "without punctuation," or "pointing") and also the pushing toward vision. It is a high-wire act that the poem itself enacts, with its graceful tercets and its single long, languorous sentence covering twenty-one lines and concluding like a child's counting game:

> And that leaves this one on the side of his
>   mountain,
> Hunched over the page, thanking his loves
>   for coming
> And keeping him company all this time.

—Christopher Benfey. "The Enigma of Arrival." *The New Republic* (March 8, 1993): pp. 36.

DAVID ST. JOHN ON THE USE OF DREAM AND MEMORY

[David St. John teaches at the University of Southern California, Los Angeles. He is the author of five books of poetry, the recipient of the Prix de Rome fellowship in literature, a Guggenheim Fellowship, The James D. Phelan Prize, the Discover/*The Nation* prize and several NEA fellowships. In this essay, he discusses the use of memory and dream to create the intimate tone and dreamscape of the poem.]

Strand's poetry has often been discussed as a hybrid of the acutely perceived "real," as in the work of a poet like Elizabeth Bishop, and of the highly speculative and imaginative verbal pageants of a poet like Wallace Stevens. Strand himself has frequently acknowledged these poetic parents, yet never has their marriage seemed more apt than under the shaded arbors of "Dark Harbor." The deceptive simplicity of Strand's lines and the exquisite eloquence of his cadences reflect an ease of intelligence unequaled since Stevens. In fact, in its abstract lyricism, "Dark Harbor's" most profound echoes seem to arise out of Stevens' gorgeous late poems, notably "Notes Towards a Supreme Fiction."

Many readers of Strand's early poems (his "Selected Poems" appeared in 1990) are accustomed to work in which the self is predicated upon a renunciation of the world, or upon a recognition of the insubstantiality of all things. Indeed, it sometimes seems that the self is barely held by the sieve of these poems. Yet Strand's early work always desires to invent its own transparency, so that a more complex psychological life might be revealed.

These attempts to pare down the self to its own essentiality gave way somewhat in Strand's most recent collection, "The Continuous Life" (1990). Where once the quotidian was banished, the elements of daily life there found celebration. Now, in "Dark Harbor," we find ourselves accompanying the poet along the course—the journey—of an artistic life. From the safety of home we begin what the speaker ironically calls "passages of greater and lesser worth," with the triple pun on "passages" of time, travel and poetry.

—David St. John "A Devotion to the Vagaries of Desire" *Los Angeles Times Book Review* Section 5 (May 9, 1993).

DAVID LEHMAN ON THE THEMATIC INFLUENCE OF WALLACE STEVENS

[David Lehman is faculty member of the graduate writing programs at Bennington College and the New

School for Social Research. He is the author of five books of poems, the editor of the Best American Poetry Series and a distinguished literary critic and editor. In this review, he likens Strand's project to Wallace Steven's "farewell to an idea."]

Favored by fortune, Mark Strand won recognition early on as one of the foremost poets of his generation. Great things were routinely expected of him. His lyrical and rhetorical gifts went together with a painter's eye and a connoisseur's disposition, as was clear from his first two collections, "Sleeping With One Eye Open" (1964) and "Reasons for Moving" (1968). In addition to poems, he wrote prose books, art books and books for children, edited anthologies and translated from the Portuguese; and he did all these things well.

Strand had no trouble mastering two of the signature styles of the late 1960s and early '70s: the surrealistic (dark or impish, sometimes dark and impish) and the Spartan (curt, austere and strict). In time, these poetic strategies would deposit him at the end of a dead-end street, and in the 1980s he entered a prolonged dry spell. I suspect that for Strand this crisis was rather like those described in Romantic odes by Wordsworth and Coleridge—a crisis of faith to be triumphantly resolved in the end by an act of affirmative imagination.

Strand snapped out of a decade-long silence with the best poems of his life—those collected in "The Continuous Life" (1990). "Dark Harbor," his new book-length poem, is continuous with its predecessor in theme and manner, and surpasses it as an act of sustained literary grace.

In "Keeping Things Whole," his most famous early poem, Strand wrote, "In a field / I am the absence / of field / This is / always the case. / Wherever I am / I am what is missing." These lines were treated by critics and commentators as the poet's cri de coeur. But in Strand's recent work, the negative presence that felt itself to be a displacement of airy molecules has prepared the way for a rich profusion of imaginings.

In "Dark Harbor" Strand remains committed to the task of negotiating, in verse, between desire and despair, possibility and fulfillment. On occasion he still resorts almost reflexively to a negating gesture ("I am writing from a place you have never been, / Where the trains don't run, and planes / Don't land"). What is new is the confidence of his speech, the extraordinary clarity with which he addresses any poet's biggest themes: love and death and aging and change.

"Dark Harbor" consists of 45 sections of varying lengths. Each can be read as an independent poem. The book is written entirely in unrhymed three-line stanzas strongly suggestive of the unit favored by Strand's acknowledged master, Wallace Stevens, in several of his great later poems. Indeed, "Dark Harbor" may be Strand's response to "The Auroras of Autumn," in which Stevens spoke his "farewell to an idea"—an idea pictured as a deserted cabin on a beach. Here is Strand on the same theme in "Dark Harbor." This is part 16 in its entirety.

"It is true, as someone has said, that in / A world without heaven all is farewell. / Whether you wave your hand or not,

"It is farewell, and if no tears come to your eyes / It Is still farewell, and if you pretend not to notice, / Hating what passes, it is still farewell.

"Farewell no matter what. And the palms as they lean / Over the green, bright lagoon, and the pelicans / Diving, and the glistening bodies of bathers resting.

"Are stages in an ultimate stillness, and the movement / Of sand, and of wind, and the secret moves of the body / Are part of the same, a simplicity that turns being

"Into an occasion for mourning, or into an occasion / Worth celebrating, for what else does one do, / Feeling the weight of the pelicans' wings.

"The density of the palms' shadows, the cells that darken / The backs of bathers? These are beyond the distortions / Of chance, beyond the evasions of music. The end

"Is enacted again and again. And we feel it / In the temptations of sleep, in the moon's ripening, / In the wine as it waits in the glass."

The artful repetition, the dramatic tempo, are characteristic of the author—as is the verbal gusto, the way lament turns into celebration and an abstract argument is superseded by the imagery supposed to illustrate it. In the ebb and flow of his three-line stanzas, Strand has found the right measure for a meditative style capable of terrific intensity and compression but also of a certain expansiveness.

"The greatest poverty is not to live in a physical world," Stevens wrote, and Strand's poetry is in some sense an elaboration of the sentiment. His work is unabashedly dedicated to the pursuit of the good life—and to the project of testing the extent to which it is possible to lead that life. One can well imagine him contemplating death on the abyss while holding a half-full wine glass on a balcony overlooking a Mediterranean beach in winter.

In "Dark Harbor" we catch glimpses of the poet celebrating "how good life / Has been and how it has culminated in this instant," lunching with his editor at Lutece, then striding along the pavement, well-fed, lanky, in his "new dark blue double-breasted suit." A poet of glamor for whom light is "the mascara of Eden," he also is a poet of romance who speaks of the "... feel of kisses blown out of heaven, / Melting the moment they land."

>—David Lehman. "Mark Strand's Farewells: Celebrating a Book-length Poem of 'sustained literary grace.'" *Chicago Tribune Books* (August 1, 1993): pp. 13.

JEFFREY DONALDSON ON THE USE OF THE ORPHEUS MYTH

> [Jeffrey Donaldson teaches poetry and American literature at McMaster University. His current projects include work in the Collected Works of Northrop Frye project. He has two books of poems and is widely published in little magazines including *The Paris Review*. In this essay-review, Donaldson posits Orpheus as the poet's representative in the landscape of the darkening harbor.]

Orpheus is the poet's representative in this landscape, as he wanders quietly with the others among nearly half of the poems collected here, asking as the light fails, how and what he should sing, how he is to be heard, where he should go, to whom he should call. Naturally, for the poet Orpheus, the darkening harbor is something more than just the geography of our historical lives, where we stand just a little offshore, trying to get away. For someone who has been to the underworld and back, our dark harbor is also the river Styx, the entrance to Hades, populated with shades of the unliving:

> ... my hand, as I lift it over the shade
> Of my body, becomes a flame pointing the way
> To a world from which no one returns, yet towards
>
> Which everyone travels....
>
> ... And the new place, the night,
> Spacious, empty, a tomb of lights, turning away,
> And going under, becoming what no one remembers. (17)

Wherever Orpheus's presence is felt, the late world that we inhabit is perceived to be in part already the underworld that it promises to become. There is something ghostly and unreal about the shades of lives we find moving about in the poems. "Our friends who lumbered from room to room / Now move like songs or meditations winding down, / Or lie about, waiting for the next good thing—/ Some news of what is going on above, / A visitor to tell them who's writing well, / Who's falling in or out of love" (45). It is difficult to tell here whether Strand is describing Orpheus's encounters in the underworld, or accounting for that analogous sense of loss and remoteness from friends that is our portion in *this* world. They are indistinguishable. There is a good deal of Milton behind all of this, the lounging of the fallen angels on the hillsides of hell (which seem strangely earthly and rural in their appearance), and Satan's cry that we ourselves are hell. Dante is here as well, who, in his representations of life in the inferno, could draw so richly from his earthly experiences. For Strand, however, the underworld of where we live, like the Hades of the pagan poets, involves no sense of judgment or punishment, but describes a condition of human nature; it is a metaphor for a psychological state that is already ours, a Hades of loss and remoteness that we already inhabit, and where "all you want is to rise out of the shade / Of yourself into the cooling blaze of a summer night / When the moon shines and the earth itself / Is covered and silent in the stoniness of its sleep" (9). This leaves us with the feeling of being liberated into our own afterlife (detached, remote, suspended in limbo, circling within ourselves), and the feeling that we have entered into the bitter promise of things as they are.

The same might be said of the landscape itself. Dante's scorching inferno and Milton's fiery "darkness visible" have become here a living dark harbor after the blaze of sunset, a world of shade and afterlight, a middle ground once again, calmer and more melancholic, in which we are at once held back and released, and find ourselves in a place and in a life that is both less and more than itself:

> Beyond the sadness—the empty restaurants,
> The empty streets, the small lamps shining
> Down on the town—I see only stretches
>
> Of ice and snow, the straight pines, the frigid moon. (19)

This is one of the most characteristic qualities of Strand's latest poetry: that paradoxical feeling we have, under western skies, that while the lights are going down the sky opens up, and that, even while we become increasingly conscious of a painful, dull, almost ascetic simplicity in the environment, there is an accompanying sense of altitude, open distance and clarity that fills it up. As objects return to themselves, they seem to become larger. Strand is one of the few American poets still reminding us that only very great artists can say the simple things. Each landscape is made up of two or three elements that are moved about in the poems like so much furniture, or they are parts of very simple sliding stage-flats (the mountain and the tree here, the harbor and the cloud there). And as with stage scenery, part of our sense of spaciousness here derives from our instant recognition that Strand's mountains and skies are largely symbolic. Like Bailey's kitchen utensils, they are chosen, not accidentally observed: their reality is ideational, and, diminished as they seem, "we have the sensation that we are seeing an arrangement that has always been and will continue to be long after we depart" (*Bailey* 18). Abstraction is itself a way of lending a place roomy clarity and permanence.

We do inhabit a closed world of darkening elements and simplified spaces, but, for a poet, the reproduction of that world in poetic terms (using simple tonal elements, coarsely conceived imagery), does not stand merely as a metaphor for something that we feel in the real world. It is an experience that the poem itself partakes of, and one that it can by its very nature make real to us. For Orpheus, the song is life; its extension is life's extension: the journey out into the dark harbor is also a journey out to the end of the poem, a journey to the end of singing. It is not unnatural, then, that he would fear the end, worry that it is no more than an end, that "the Beyond is just a beyond" (and not an underworld in which he can charm the gods with his music), and that his own voice will not last: "... will I have proved that whatever I love / Is unbearable, that the views of Lethe will never / Improve, that whatever I sing is a blank?" (43). The poems themselves seem self-conscious of their own closed space: they so often quietly invoke, just as they end, the whole problem of ending and limitation. I have already quoted the end of "The End" in *The Continuous Life*. Here are a few concluding lines from *Dark Harbor*: "for the ash / Of the body is worthless and goes only so far" (3); "... the particular way our voices / Erased all signs of the sorrow that had been, / Its violence, its terrible omens of the end" (13); "an understanding that remains unfinished, unentire, / Largely imperfect so long as it lasts" (34); "a fragment, a piece of a larger intention, that is all" (41). It almost seems that as the poem concludes it cannot help but draw discreet attention to the fact of its own imminent extinction, with a note of lamentation or complaint in the phrases "goes only so far," "omens of the end," "so long as it lasts," and "that is all." Strand feels this limitation as a palpable reality of the poem itself, but using something very like picture windows on the interior walls, he also shows the way out beyond it. Here, in the proem to the book, he announces his method:

> "This is the way," he continued as he watched
> For the great space that he felt sure
>
> Would open before him, a stark sea over which
> The turbulent sky would drop the shadowy shapes
> Of its song, and he would move his arms
>
> And begin to mark, almost as a painter would,
> The passages of greater and lesser worth, the silken
> Tropes and calls to this or that, coarsely conceived,
>
> Echoing and blasting all around. (vii)

—Jeffrey Donaldson. "Still Life of Mark Strand's Darkening Harbor." *Dalhousie Review* 74:1 (Spring 1994): pp. 117–18.

RICHARD TILLINGHAST ON STRAND'S USE OF AND PLACE WITHIN THE WESTERN CANON

[Richard Tillinghast teaches in the Master of Fine Arts program at the University of Michigan. He is the author of seven books of poetry, a travel writer, book reviewer, Director of The Poet's House in Ireland and a memoirist. In this review, Tillinghast reveals the origins of many of Strand's poetic devices.]

This poetry has all of Strand's accustomed smoothness, but the voice can erupt into surprisingly heartfelt utterances. In VIII he sets us up with a swiftly rendered scene that smacks of hearty well-being where the poet goes "out tonight / In my new dark blue double-breasted suit" to "sit in a restaurant with a bowl // Of soup before me to celebrate how good life / Has been and how it has culminated in this instant." Then in a swift turnabout we find ourselves in a Baudelairean world confronting Strand's muse, addressed ironically and disturbingly: "I love your gold teeth and your dyed hair—/ A little green, a little yellow—and your weight, / Which is finally up where we never thought / It would be." It is a dramatic moment that places Strand firmly in the line of serious European poetry with roots in the French nineteenth century: "O my partner, my beautiful death, / My black paradise, my fusty intoxicant, // My symbolist muse, give me your breast / Or your hand or your tongue" (XIV). "The ship has been held in the harbor" takes the reader back to "Le Bateau Ivre" of Rimbaud and other modern works that play on the metaphor of a ship sailing out into the unknown. The gravity of the sequence is accomplished not only by its lofty subject matter but also by its alliteration and extended phrasing: "A long time has passed and yet it seems / Like yesterday, in the midmost moment of summer." The line is often, as in the second of these two, iambic pentameter. (...)

Dark Harbor is a treasure of different ploys, shifts in tone, changes in genre. XVII, for instance, is a harvest poem that owes something to Keats's "Ode to Autumn," where "Someone has fallen asleep on a boxcar of turnips." XXII is a sexual comedy: "Madame X begged to be relieved / Of a sexual pain that had my name / Written all over it." XXXI reprises a similar scene, this time in a cabin in Labrador. The figure of Orpheus appears in a couple of poems late in the book, touching on the role of poetry in the world: "Rivers, mountains, animals, all find their true place, // But only while Orpheus sings. When the song is over / The world resumes its old flaws."

—Richard Tillinghast. "Review." *Poetry* (August 1995): pp. 293–4

CHRISTOPHER R. MILLER ON THE COMPARISON BETWEEN *DARK HARBOR* AND STEVENS' "WAVING ADIEU, ADIEU, ADIEU"

[Christopher R. Miller is an Assistant Professor of English at Yale University. He has published articles on Coleridge and a number of 20-century American poets. In this essay, he makes explicit comparisons between the two poems, citing "inventions of farewell" a Stevens phrase, as fundamental to understanding Strand's poetics.]

Strand wrote in his most overtly Stevensian vein in the sequence *Dark Harbor*, which consists of what might be called, in Stevens' phrase, "inventions of farewell" (*CP* 432). Several vignettes address seasonal change in ways that implicitly ask how to write a season-poem after Stevens. In one, Strand offers a brief credence of summer, set in a "dark harbor" indeed—a tropical seascape in which sybaritic contentment is shadowed by ultimate thoughts of death, expressed in Stevens' own idiom and characteristic tercets:

> It is true, as someone has said, that in
> A world without heaven all is farewell.
> Whether you wave your hand or not,
>
> It is farewell, and if no tears come to your eyes
> It is still farewell, and if you pretend not to notice,
> Hating what passes, it is still farewell. (DH 18)

"Someone" has said this, more or less, in "Waving Adieu, Adieu, Adieu":

> That would be waving and that would be crying,
> Crying and shouting and meaning farewell,
> Farewell in the eyes and farewell at the centre,
> Just to stand still without moving a hand.
>
> In a world without heaven to follow, the stops
> Would be endings, more poignant than partings,
>   profounder,
> And that would be saying farewell, repeating farewell,
> Just to be there and just to behold. (*CP* 127)

Strand renders Stevens' "Waving Adieu" even more Stevensian: he expresses the flux of existence in sublime abstractions, finds serene stasis behind motion. All elements of the scene—leaning palms, diving pelicans, glistening bathers—are "stages in an ultimate stillness"; the dark materiality of the world is "beyond the distortions / Of chance." Whereas Stevens' poem begins as a scherzo, with its giddy, anapestic surges, Strand's maintains its meditative poise throughout. In comparing the two variations on a theme of "adieu," we see the poets' distinct temperaments. Stevens' most solemn inventions of farewell often contain a countersong of jubilance, famously expressed by the couplet in "Esthétique du Mal": "Natives of poverty, children of malheur, / The gaiety of language is our seigneur" (*CP* 322). Strand's poems, on the other hand, speak a more austere language.

I have suggested that Strand does not quite fit the category of "strong poet" as Bloom defines it; but in this poem, Strand does adopt a strong stance toward Stevens in turning him into an anonymous "someone," a flash of voice coming momentarily into consciousness. Stevens' words, like the tropes of breath and whiteness, serve as the keynote for a meditation. Is Strand merely illustrating a Stevensian theme, or does he swerve from his predecessor in some way? Since he begins with the concessive phrase, "It is true," we would expect him to introduce the qualification of a "but" or an "and yet," but he seems intent instead on illustrating Stevens' premise, visualizing a setting for it. Toward the end, Strand introduces a choice of sorts: in a world without heaven, mere being becomes "an occasion for mourning" or "an occasion / Worth celebrating," and Strand refuses to arbitrate between these possibilities beyond suggesting that there are no others. The poem turns, finally, on a rhetorical question and a restatement of idea:

> for what else does one do,
> Feeling the weight of the pelicans' wings,
>
> The density of the palms' shadows, the cells that darken
> The backs of bathers? These are beyond the distortions
> Of chance, beyond the evasions of music. The end
>
> Is enacted again. And we feel it
> In the temptations of sleep, in the moon's ripening,
> In the wine as it waits in the glass. (DH 18)

How does one end a poem that begins with "farewell"? Both poets ask questions, but they ask different kinds, and in different orders. Strand's suggests a starkly binary choice between mourning and celebrating earthly mutability. Without preferring one or the other, Strand simply offers further intimations of mortality—tempting sleep, waxing moon, waiting wine—that echo Stevens' own infinitives of farewell ("to sip / One's cup and never to say a word, / Or to sleep or just to lie there still"). Stevens' adieux, however, lead to a different question: "Ever-jubilant, / What is there here but weather, what spirit / Have I except it comes from the sun?" (*CP* 128). In Stevens' symbolic lexicon, the sun is the archetypal First Idea, a constant presence in the poetry, from the "savage of fire" of "Gubbinal" to the "battered panache" of "Not Ideas about the Thing but the Thing Itself." It is the hypothetical divinity to which the worshippers in "Sunday Morning" chant "boisterous devotion"; the "spaciousness and light / In which the body walks and is deceived" in "Anatomy of Monotony"; the "opulent" vandal of "A Postcard from the Volcano" that smears the abandoned house with gilt graffiti. In Strand's poem, however, the sun becomes yet another intimation of mortality, the energy that shatters chromosomes and causes skin cancer. Strand, who does not share Stevens' mythopoetic imagination, seems to suggest a counter-sublime here: the sun as destroyer rather than creator.

—Christopher R. Miller. "Mark Strand's Inventions of Farewell." *The Wallace Stevens Journal* 24:2 (Fall 2000): pp. 143–44.

JAMES F. NICOSIA: MARSYAS IN *DARK HARBOR*

[Jim Nicosia is an independent scholar who has taught at several schools in the northern New Jersey area.]

In an atypical Strandian twist that can be viewed in a Freudian light, the precursor is transformed, one might say, into the poet's father in order that this poet can kill his father. Yet, perspective becomes skewed here, as well, for poet and precursor begin to become one and the same. When the speaker is shown painting a gun into the precursor's hand and pointing it at "the one who assumed / The responsibility of watching" (24–25), it becomes difficult to decipher who that "one who assumed" is. Indeed, it seems to be both men, and attempting to distinguish the shooter from the victim seems immaterial; when the trigger is pulled, neither dies. Instead, "something falls, / A fragment, a piece of a larger intention, that is all" (26–27). The poetic noise uttered at the conclusion of part XXXVIII then leaves us with another Strandian silence that must be confronted, and is, in the following segment. In part XXXIX, the speaker seems to begin again, and takes a deep breath in preparation for the final stages of this monumental poem. He begins in a state of uncertainty, issuing a sentence fragment that hesitantly declares his intention to write without actually beginning the poem (of course, he *has* begun, for the two stanzas *are* present, yet, in their assertion that they *will* begin a poem, they thus declare the *absence* of poem).

With the struggle to recapture the poet's voice thus brought to the fore again, Strand declares, "Today I shall consider Marsyas," the mythological figure flayed after challenging Apollo to a musical contest (2–3). The pieces that remain at the end of part XXXVIII are picked up here as the remains of Marsyas, useless items again needed by the poet to reconstruct something of the world of the past—even if that world is the previous poem. Again, the poem finds the speaker wondering whether or not he should bother to try, whether the effort is worth expending.

Benfey is correct to note that "The company of poets [to which Strand seeks to belong] can be intimidating, ... and in *Dark Harbor* this fear is embodied in the figure of Marsyas" (36). His further assumption, however, that "the link" in this poem "is clearly that of fear of not being good enough, the writer's 'block' that is both obstacle and punishment" overlooks the redemption that ends the poem (36). In Strand's familiar elegiac style, the poem spirals upward. He "considers" Marsyas in the first, third and fourth stanzas, seemingly lamenting that poet's—and, by extension, *this* poet's—fate. Yet, in each *re*consideration, Strand brings something new to the mix, and thus rebuilds the poet in the making. By the time the poem ends, it exhibits a certain revitalization.

The grieving that dominates the early moments of this segment gives way to a reuse of this *materia poetica* called Marsyas. Strand transforms his flayed flesh into "the flesh of light, / Which is fed to onlookers centuries later" (12–13). The poetic influence of Marsyas is felt by, of course, Strand the "onlooker," who then repays Marsyas with the poem at the same time as he rewrites Marsyas. "Can this be the cost of encompassing pain?" this speaker now asks (14), as much of himself as of his predecessor. He, too, has felt the pain of "a long silence" (15), and attempts to use the experience as a unifying feature for him and his predecessor. Yet, the "correct" answer requires some reconsideration, and a useful Strandian conjunction: "Or is a body scraped from the bone of experience, the chart of suffering / To be read in such ways that all flesh might be redeemed, / At least for the moment, the moment it passes into song?" (19–21). Yes, for a moment, there is redemption, there is hope, in the singing—that tiny instant of engagement. As Spiegelman says, "Hopefulness, even muted, is hopefulness still" (135).

Yet, if part XXXIX ends with an acknowledgment that the poet can be redeemed in the moment he translates his experience into song, that song, of course, ends at the poem's conclusion, and the new poem, XL, begins after the latest silence. It necessarily must address loss, for the "moment" of segment XXXIX has passed. And now, he asks,

> How can I sing when I haven't the heart, or the hope
> That something of paradise persists in my song,
> That a touch of those long afternoons of summer . . .
> Will find a home in yet another imagined place? (1–5)

The other imagined place is, of course, in the mind of the reader. His incessant goal as poet: eternal value for his creation. "[W]ill I have proved / That I live against time," he asks (8–9). Or is the final answer: "whatever I sing is a blank?" (12). Though the indecision is maddening, it is the indecision that is the subject of his writing, and *as* the subject of his writing, it is the indecision that *keeps* him writing. It is a painful temporary redemption for this poet, indeed, and the concluding quintet of poems does its utmost to speak up against the perpetual fear of the speaking being ineffectual.

Segment XLI's solution to the meaninglessness of "the night

sky" (2), to the realization that "I have no idea / Of what I see" (2–3), and to the number of the stars being "far beyond / What I can reckon" (4–5), is a "who knows," that seems to speak more as a "who cares?" (13). This poet speaks, he now says, because he must speak—of his joys, of his fears, of his inability to speak, and of his need to speak. Where the poem goes from there is now immaterial in the face of the poet's requirement to write. Of tomorrow, he says, "We are already travelling faster than our / Apparent stillness can stand, and if it keeps up / You will be light-years away by the time I speak" (13–15). Indeed, this segment's point of utterance is already far removed from the reader's point of reading. The poet's ability to affect the reader has long ended, and, in the scheme of real time, several poems already have been penned between this one and the reader's reception of it.

Time continues to race past unconcerned with the world's human inhabitants in segment XLII, and now none of it matters to the poet, or so he says. Marsyas, the hero of segment XXXIX, has been "asleep for centuries" (9), and "Arion, whose gaudy music drove the Phrygians wild, / Hasn't spoken in a hundred years" (10–11). Both are dead, and the poet seems sure of this one "truth": "Soon the song deserts its maker" (12). Yet, Strand seems to be establishing a potential for union by linking these early poets in their silence. Hints are present when he says, "The airy demon dies, and others come along" (13). The others include himself, and though no union is established just yet, the experienced Strand reader can see it just around the corner, in the next poem. Surely, while there is no celebration here, when Strand says, "A different kind of dark invades the autumn woods, / A different sound sends lovers packing into sleep" (14-15), it is still a sound of poets—new poets such as himself. Likewise, a line like "The air is full of anguish" contains little to relish (16), yet it *is* full of the anguish of the new poets. As for tomorrow, this poet seems to leave it where it is—in that unreachable realm expressed in the previous segment of *Dark Harbor*. He now says, "The Beyond is *merely* beyond, / A melancholy place of failed and fallen stars" (17–18, italics mine).

And so, with the old poets discussed and put to rest, part XLIII begins to establish some continuity between poets.

Though the piano music is no longer played, and the players are also gone, Strand links Jules Laforgue and Wallace Stevens in an extension of the torch-passing theme of the previous poem. He resurrects these poets and their poems in his reconsideration of them, but, as in the previous segments, he ends without resurrecting poetry to a place of honor. The connective bridge sustained here again is poetry's mutability: "The snows have come, and the black shapes of the pianos / Are sleeping and cannot be roused, like the girls themselves / Who have gone, and the leaves, and all that was just here" (13–15). Strand's own poem ("all that was just here") is unified with the poets who created the precursor poems, and their poems (the leaves) themselves. Though they "cannot be roused," there are commonalities being established in these final segments, ultimately which will be tied together in the celebration of the final segment's song. But for now, "all that was just here," the momentary salvation experienced in the writing of *this* poem, as well as all the delight achieved from the previous poems and their poets, are gone.

Part XLIV begins in a reminiscence of earlier days and ends in a recognition of the sea as an enduring, generative force that awed the speaker as a child and has intimidated the poet as an adult, for it was the enduring force he wished his poetry could be. Indeed, *Dark Harbor* ends at the sea, considering the past, the same place from where the Proem was issued. For the speaker as a child, there was also something frightening about the power of the sea's loud voice. But "now years later / It is the sound as well as its size that I love" (8–9). Indeed, the sea has both the voice and the endurance that the poet, that *every* poet, seeks so fervently. And from the dawn of man, the sea has been speaking *to* these poets. Here, this poet has lost his voice "in my inland exile among the mountains" (10).

Ah, those mountains from part XXXII, those same mountains that have intimidated him into submission, those same mountains that separate him from his angel-poets in part XXVII. They, too, are enduring, but they do not speak. Ironically, the speaker now admires the ocean's changeability. Like the poet—or, perhaps more accurately, like the poet wishes to be—the ocean creates and destroys and is varied in its appearance from day to day, wave to wave, moment to moment.

This poet's mountains: "do not change except for the light / That colors them or the snows that make them remote / Or the clouds that lift them, so they appear much higher / Than they are" (11–14). The ocean is the imagination at its strongest, capable of effecting change. This poet's mountains "are acted upon and have none / Of the mystery of the sea that generates its own changes" (14–15). And this eternal sea cries, too. These are the cries the poet now recognizes as a poetic need for him, as well. Gone are the days of childhood. Now, despite the futility of his situation—or *because* of the futility of his situation—as mere mortal, he must face the silence, face death, face the insecurity of the future:

> [I]n those days what did I know of the pleasures of loss,
> Of the abyss coming close with its hisses
> And storms, a great watery animal breaking itself on the rocks,
>
> Sending up stars of salt, loud clouds of spume. (19–22)

This poet now recognizes that poetry is not merely a bulwark against pain and suffering. Now he recognizes that loss is a *source* of poetry, as well. Instead of railing against the darknesses that exist before and after the poetic invention, the poet now focuses upon that invention that *does*, regardless of its origins and its fate, exist.

Which brings us to segment XLV, which ends *Dark Harbor* by radiating from itself, calling out to the future and to the past "masters" of poetry. Finally, it presents that communion for Strand among the community of poets. This concluding poem-within-a-poem originates in a primal, "misty" scene, one that seems to be left over just as the great forgetters of "Always," from Strand's *The Continuous Life*, are completing their erasure of the world. The speaker discovers "Groups of souls, wrapped in cloaks" (3) in the fields. This place reminds the speaker of another place, where a stranger who mysteriously recognizes him:

> Approached, saying there were many poets
> Wandering around who wished to be alive again.
> They were ready to say the words they had been unable to say—

Words whose absence had been the silence of love,
Of pain, and even of pleasure" (10–14)

Surely, these are not those inspirational poets wishing to return to earth, the place of love. More likely they are the "lazy poets" of Strand's "The History of Poetry," who, no longer having the power to create that they had on earth, have gathered together to mourn missed opportunity and to unlearn their habits. For they have a new teacher now, and they are learning to speak of the imagination. They have found communion, discovered that "the golden lights of sunset / And sunrise are one and the same" (18–19). Their teacher: "an angel, one of the good ones, about to sing" (21).

Yet, upon closer scrutiny, perhaps, Strand is saying, this is the fate of all poets once they have been defeated by death. In the face of such eternal silence, Strand's hedging throughout the poem appears to be a waste of effort. Here, he seems to recognize that there will be plenty of time for silence. Any words unsaid now will be regretted in the long silence after the imagination has been abandoned, after *life* has ceased. The "Someone, / who claimed to have known me years before" (8–9)—this mysterious speaker within the speaker's poem—has a lesson to teach. He is a liaison between the world of the now-silenced precursor poets and the living poet. It is he who summons the good angel to speak to his now-rapt audience, and the silence that ends the poem is the most promising of all silences, for it awaits the angel's impending poem. Rarely has a Strand book ended with as forward-looking and promising a hope as now found within the figure of an angel—the imagination that Stevens calls "the necessary angel"—hovering over this dark scene, right at the moment when the song is about to be sung. Few things are more promising than the promise of song. And if we indeed see the poem as circular—or at least spoken in both directions—the promise bears itself out in this most successful work of art, this angel-song.

Lived experience between the bookends of darkness
Critics disagree on the tone of *Dark Harbor*. Tillinghast

remarks that Strand presents a sincerity of emotion in *Dark Harbor*, noting an "elevated, classical tone that unifies its disparate parts" (292–293). Spiegelman disunites the poem by accurately identifying the "faux-naif tone" of certain poems (136). Benfey reminds that Strand also exhibits startlingly playful brashness in segments such as XIX, XXII and XXIII.

In general, Strand also appears in different form to different people. Those with a penchant for European literature see Frenchmen Baudelaire, Rimbaud and German Rilke in Strand, and for good reason. Those who specialize in British Romanticism, see in him Keats and Wordsworth, again with well-founded opinions. It would be remiss to ignore the Dante-esque quality of the three-line stanzas of *Dark Harbor*. And yet, there are a few critics to correctly note his affinity with Latin American poets, who he has studied and translated. On one thing, critics (other than Gregerson, that is) seem to agree: his work is oddly familiar despite the apparent originality of its bluntness in the face of the world's horrors. Pinsky may not have been entirely complementary when saying, "Strand is an original writer, but not of the kind who challenges our idea of poetry. He confirms that idea, rather than enlarging it" (300-1), but few poets can hope to reach the level of imaginative achievement necessary to "confirm" our idea of poetry as compellingly—and, I might add, definitively—as he does. Indeed, Strand is a well-read writer who seems unafraid to reconsider any of his precursors. It is this universality of influence that probably identifies the accuracy of Spiegelman's contention, "Many of Strand's elegiac notes sound reassuring rather than threatening, precisely because of the familiarity of their tone" (135). Remarkably, they seem familiar to everyone, for different reasons.

While given labels like confessionalist, surrealist, fantasist and postmodernist, Strand is a serious poet in the Romantic tradition contemplating and contending with the possibilities of poetry in a world where faith in religion and most other institutions have been lost. Without trying to oversimplify, a chart can be drawn marking the increasing strength of the imagination throughout Strand's career. That chart has its peaks and valleys, but on the whole, the poet's voice grows louder in its capacity to call forth an imaginative vision. In *Dark Harbor*, Strand charts the whole territory anew, summarizing the growth of a poet from *ephebe* to strong poet. In paying close attention to what the poems do and how they do it, we have hopefully achieved what Henri Cole rightly calls "the cumulative effect" of Strand's vision. Indeed, it is our contention that *Dark Harbor* intends to produce such a cumulative effect. Despite its variations, it is a singleminded poem aimed at expressing the obstacles presented to the contemporary poet, and in particular, an aging contemporary poet. As Spiegelman says, "Wedding his cool Stevensian side to a more strapping Whitmanian feeling for the sea and its combination of terror and maternal comfort, Strand acknowledges certain adult emotions of which the young are deprived" (135). Ultimately, *Dark Harbor* asserts the vitality of "poetry itself, the naked poem, the imagination manifesting itself in its domination of words" (Stevens *Imaginary* viii).

In our travels through this assertion of the imagination, we have run into many repeating images—primitive and privative absences and darknesses, the desire for safe haven amid the world's whirlwinds, the assertion of the imaginative gesture as temporarily redeeming. Ultimately, what *Dark Harbor* comes down to is the celebration of the subjectively meaningful action in the face of an apathetic world. In imagining the poem, Strand continually reinvents himself in a place of poets, that we, too, are given when we accompany him. And in imagining the poem, he provides for himself and his reader temporary joy. Although Strand's imaginative powers have grown steadily from the weak attempts to stave off the storms of *Sleeping with One Eye Open*, to the multiple-layered creative powers of *Dark Harbor*, for now, Strand is still asking his blank page, "Where, where in Heaven am I?" And for now, even if the imagination does not sustain, "Still, we feel better for trying."

—James F. Nicosia. "Marsyas in *Dark Harbor*" appears for the first time in this publication. © 2003 James F. Nicosia.

WORKS BY
Mark Strand

Sleeping with One Eye Open, 1964.
Reasons for Moving: Poems, 1968.
The Contemporary American Poets: American Poetry Since 1940 (editor), 1968.
Darker: Poems, 1970.
New Poetry of Mexico (edited with Octavio Paz), 1970.
18 Poems from the Quechua (edited and translated by Strand), 1971.
The Story of Our Lives, 1973.
The Owl's Insomnia (translation of Rafael Alberti), 1973.
The Sargeantville Notebook, 1974.
Another Republic: 17 European and South American Writers (edited with Charles Simic), 1976.
Souvenir of the Ancient World (translation of Carlos Drummond de Andrade), 1976.
Elegy for My Father, 1978.
The Late Hour, 1978.
The Monument, 1978.
Selected Poems, 1980.
The Planet of Lost Things, 1982.
Claims for Poetry (contributor, edited by Donald Hall).
The Night Book, 1983.
Art of the Real, 1983.
Mr. and Mrs. Baby and Other Stories, 1985.
Traveling in the Family (translation of Carlos Drummond de Andrade with Thomas Colchie) 1986.
Rembrandt Takes a Walk, 1986.
William Bailey, 1987.

The Continuous Life, 1990.
New Poems, 1990.
The Monument, 1991.
The Best American Poetry 1991 (guest editor), 1991.
Reasons for Moving, Darker, and the Sargeantville Notebook, 1992.
Dark Harbor: A Poem, 1993.
Within This Garden: Photographs by Ruth Thorne-Thomsen (contributor), 1993.
Golden Ecco Anthology (editor), 1994.
Hopper, 1994.
These Rare Lands: Images of America's National Parks, 1997.
Blizzard of One: Poems, 1998.
The Weather of Words: Poetic Invention, 2000.
The Making of a Poem: A Norton Anthology of Poetic Forms (edited with Eavan Boland), 2000.

WORKS ABOUT
Mark Strand

Aaron, Jonathan. "About Mark Strand: A Profile," *Ploughshares* (Winter 1995–96): pp. 202–206.

"A Conversation with Mark Strand," *Ohio Review*, 13 (Winter 1972): pp. 54–71.

Bacchilega, Christine. "An Interview with Mark Strand," *The Missouri Review* 4:3 (1981): pp. 51–64.

Benfey, Christopher. "The Enigma of Arrival," *The New Republic* (March 8, 1993): pp. 34–7.

Bensko, John. "Reflexive Narration in Contemporary American Poetry: Some Examples from Mark Strand, John Ashberry, Norman Dubie, and Louis Simpson," *The Journal of Narrative Technique* 16:2 (Spring 1986): pp. 81–96.

Berger, Charles. "Reading as Poets Read: Following Mark Strand," *Philosophy and Literature* 20: 1 (1996): pp. 177–88.

Birkerts, Sven. "The Art of Absence," *The New Republic* (December 17, 1990): pp. 36–38.

Bloom, Harold. "Death and Radiant Peripheries: Mark Strand and A.R. Ammons," *Southern Review* (Winter 1972): pp. 133-41.

Brennan, Matthew. "Mark Strand's 'For Her,'" *Notes on Contemporary Literature* 13 (January 1983): pp. 11–12.

Byrne, Edward. "Weather Watch: Mark Strand's *The Weather of Words*." *Valparaiso Poetry Review: Contemporary Poetry and Poetics* II: 2 (Spring/Summer 2000): www.valpo.edu/english/vprv2n2.html.

Cavalieri, Grace. "Mark Strand: An Interview," *American Poetry Review* 23:4 (1994): pp. 39–41.

Cole, Henri. Review. *Poetry* (April 1991): pp. 54–7.

Coleman, Jane Candia. Reviews. *Western American Literature* (Summer 1991): pp. 178–9.

Coles, Katherine. "In the Presence of America: A Conversation with Mark Strand: An Interview," *WeberStudies: An Interdisciplinary Humanities Journal* 9:3 (1992): pp. 8–28.

Contemporary Literary Criticism, Gale, Volume 6, 1976, Volume 18, 1981, Volume 41, 1987, Volume 71, 1992.

Cooper, Philip. "The Waiting Dark: Talking to Mark Strand," *Hollins Critic* 21 (October 1984): pp. 1–7.

Corn, Alfred. "Plural Perspectives, Heightened Perceptions," *The New York Review of Books*, March 24, 1991.

Crenner, James. "Mark Strand: Darker," *Seneca Review*, 2 (April 1971): 87–97.

Dobyns, Stephen. "Penetrable and Impenetrable," *North American Review* 257:2 (1972): pp. 57–9.

Donaldson, Jeffrey. "The Still Life of Mark Strand's Darkening Harbor," *Dalhousie Review* 74:1 (Spring 1994): pp. 110–124.

Gregerson, Linda. "Negative Capability (Mark Strand)," *Negative Capability: Contemporary American Poetry*. Ann Arbor: University of Michigan Press, 2001: pp. 5–29. Originally in *Parnassus: Poetry in Review* 9:2 (1981): 90–114.

Hoff, James. "Borges: Influences and References," *The Modern Word* (www.themodernword.com/borges/borges_infl_strand.html)

Howard, Richard. "Mark Strand," *Alone with America: Essays on the Art of Poetry Since 1950, Enlarged Edition*. New York: Atheneum, 1980: pp. 589–602.

Jackson, Richard. "Charles Simic and Mark Strand: The Presence of Absence," *Contemporary Literature* 21 (1980): pp. 136–45.

Kinzie, Mary. "Through the Looking Glass: The Romance of the Perceptual in Contemporary Poetry," *Ploughshares* (Spring 1979): pp. 202–241.

Kirby, David. *Mark Strand and the Poet's Place in Contemporary Culture.* Columbia and London: University of Missouri Press, 1990.

Lehman, David. "Mark Strand's Farewells: Celebrating a book of 'sustained literary grace'," *Chicago Tribune Books,* August 1, 1993, pp. 13.

Lieberman, Laurence. "Mark Strand: The Book of Mourning." *Beyond the Muse of Memory: Essays on Contemporary American Poets.* Columbia and London: University of Missouri Press, 1995. pp. 218-230. Originally appeared in *The Yale Review* (1968).

Maddox, Carolyn. "The Weather of Words: Poetic Invention," *Antioch Review* 59:1 (Winter 2001): pp.120.

Maio, Samuel. "The Self-Effacing Mode," *Creating Another Self: Voice in Modern American Personal Poetry.* Kirksville: Thomas Jefferson University Press, 1995: pp.163–224.

Manguso, Sarah. "Where is that boy?" *Iowa Review* 29:2 (Fall 1999): pp. 168–171.

"Mark Strand," *Contemporary Authors Online.* The Gale Group, 2001. www.galenet.com.

Martz, Louis L. "Recent Poetry: Visions and Revision," *Yale Review* 60 (1971): pp. 403–417.

McClanahan, Thomas. *Dictionary of Literary Biography, Volume 5: American Poets Since World War II, First Series.* A Bruccoli Clark Layman Book. Ed. Donald J. Greiner, University of South Carolina. The Gale Group, 1980. pp. 303–309. www.galenet.com. pp. 6.

Miller, Christopher R. "Mark Strand's Inventions of Farewell," *The Wallace Stevens Journal* 24:2 (Fall 2001): pp. 135–150

Miklitsch, Robert. "Beginnings and Endings: Mark Strand's 'The Untelling,'" *Literary Review* 21 (1977-78): pp. 357–73.

Oakes, Elizabeth. "'To Hold Them in Solution, Unsolved': The Ethic of Wholeness in Four Contemporary Poems." *REAL, The Journal of Liberal Arts* 25:1 (2000): pp. 49–59.

Olsen, Lance. "The Country Nobody Visits: The Varieties of Fantasy in Strand's Poetry," *The Shape of the Fantastic: Selected Essays from the Seventh International Conference on the Fantastic in the Arts*. Greenwood Press, Westport: 1990: pp. 3–8.

Plumly, Stanley. "From the New Poetry Handbook." *Ohio Review* 13:1 (1971): pp. 74–80.

Shawn, Wallace. "The Art of Poetry LXXVII: Mark Strand," *The Paris Review* 148 (1998): pp. 146–178.

Sheehan, Donald. "Varieties of Technique: Seven Recent Books of American Poetry," *Contemporary Literature* X (Spring 1969): pp. 284–302.

St. John, David. "'A Devotion to the Vagaries of Desire,'" *Los Angeles Times Book Review*. May 9, 1993.

Stillinger, Jack. "Wordsworth, Coleridge and the Shaggy Dog: The Novelty of *Lyrical Ballads (1798)*." *Wordsworth Circle* 31:2 (2000): pp. 70–6.

Stitt, Peter. "Engagements with Reality," *The Georgia Review* vol. 35: 4 (Winter 1981): pp. 874–882.

_____. "Stages of Reality: The Mind/Body Problem in Contemporary Poetry," *The Georgia Review* 37:1 (Spring 1983): pp. 201–210.

Strand, Mark. "Narrative Poetry," *Ploughshares* 12:3 (Fall 1986): pp. 13–4.

Thomas, Bill. "What's a Poet Laureate to Do?" *Los Angeles Times Magazine*, January 13, 1991: pp. 14.

Tillinghast, Richard. Review. *Poetry* (August 1995): pp. 292–295.

Village Voice. April 30, 1985: pp. 47.

Vine, Richard and Robert von Hallberg. "A Conversation with Mark Strand," *Chicago Review* 28:4 (Spring 1977): pp. 130–140.

ACKNOWLEDGMENTS

"Negative Capability" by Linda Gregerson. From *Negative Capability: Contemporary American Poetry* (Ann Arbor, University of Michigan Press, 2001.): pp. 5–29. Originally appeared in *Parnassus: Poetry in Review* 9:2 (1981): 90–114. © 2001 by University of Michigan Press. Reprinted by permission.

"Mark Strand" by Thomas McClanahan. From *Dictionary of Literary Biography, Volume 5: American Poets Since World War II, First Series*, Ed. Donald J. Greiner. (The Gale Group, 1980): 303–309. ©1980 by The Gale Group. Reprinted by permission of the Gale Group.

"Stages of Reality: The Mind/Body Problem in Contemporary Poetry" by Peter Stitt. From *The Georgia Review* 37: 1 (Spring 1983): 201–210. © 1983 by *The Georgia Review*. Reprinted by permission.

"Reflexive Narration in Contemporary American Poetry" by John Bensko. From *The Journal of Narrative Technique* 16:2 (Spring 1986): pp. 81–96. © 1986 by *The Journal of Narrative Technique*. Reprinted by permission.

Reprinted from *Mark Strand and the Poet's Place in Contemporary Culture* by David Kirby, by permission of the University of Missouri Press. © 1990 by the curators of the University of Missouri.

"The Art of Absence" by Sven Birkerts. From *The New Republic* 3, 961 (December 17, 1990): pp. 37. © 1990 by *The New Republic*. Reprinted by permission.

"Mark Strand: 'The Mirror Was Nothing Without You'" by Richard Howard. From *Alone with America: Essays on the Art of Poetry in the United States Since 1950, Enlarged Edition* (New York, Atheneum: 1980): pp. 596–597. © 1980 by Atheneum. Reprinted by permission.

"Dark and Radiant Peripheries: Mark Strand and A. R. Ammons" by Harold Bloom. From *Southern Review* (Winter 1972): pp. 133–41. © 1972 by the *Southern Review*. Reprinted by permission.

"Stages of Reality: The Mind/Body Problem in Contemporary Poetry" by Peter Stitt. From *The Georgia Review* 37: 1 (Spring 1983): pp. 202. © 1983 by *The Georgia Review*. Reprinted by permission.

Reprinted from *Beyond the Muse of Memory: Essays on Contemporary American Poets* by Lawrence Liebermann, by permission of the University of Missouri Press. © 1995 by the curators of the University of Missouri.

"Weather Watch: Mark Strand's *The Weather of Words*" by Edward Byrne. From *Valparaiso Poetry Review: Contemporary Poetry and Poetics* II: 2 (Spring/Summer 2000): www.valpo.edu/english/vprv2n2.html. © 2000 by *Valparaiso Poetry Review*. Reprinted by permission.

"The Enigma of Arrival" by Christopher Benfrey. From *The New Republic* (March 8, 1993): pp. 36. © 1993 by *The New Republic*. Reprinted by permission.

"A Devotion to the Vagaries of Desire" by David St. John. From *Los Angeles Times Book Review* Section 5 (May 9, 1993). © 1993 by *Los Angeles Times Book Review*. Reprinted by permission.

"Mark Strand's Farewells: Celebrating a Book-length Poem of 'sustained literary grace'" by David Lehman. From *Chicago Tribune Books* (August 1, 1993): pp. 13. © 1993 by *Chicago Tribune Books*. Reprinted by permission.

"Still Life of Mark Strand's Darkening Harbor" by Jeffrey Donaldson. From *Dalhousie Review* 74:1 (Spring 1994): pp. 117–18. © 1994 by *Dalhousie Review*. Reprinted by permission.

"Review" by Richard Tillinghast. From *Poetry* (August 1995): pp. 293–4. © 1995 by *Poetry*. Reprinted by permission.

"Mark Strand's Inventions of Farewell" by Christopher R. Miller. From *The Wallace Stevens Journal* 24:2 (Fall 2000): pp. 143–44. © 2000 by *The Wallace Stevens Journal*. Reprinted by permission.

"Marsyas in *Dark Harbor*" by James F. Nicosia. © 2003 by James F. Nicosia. Reprinted by permission.

INDEX OF
Themes and Ideas

"A BLIZZARD OF ONE," 55

DANTE, 13, 63, 70, 83

"DARK HARBOR," 57–84; ars poetica in, 62–64; critical analysis on, 57–61; critical views on, 10, 13, 42, 62–84; marsyas in, 76–84; memory and dream in, 64–65; Orpheus in, 68–72; poetic devices in, 72–73; redemption in, 57; Stevens' "Farewell to an Idea," 66–68; Stevens' "Waving Adieu, adieu, adieu," 73–76

"ELEGY FOR MY FATHER," 42–56; affirmation of life in, 48–50; critical analysis of, 42–45; critical views on, 46–56; loss of self in, 50–53; precursor to "A Blizzard of One," 55–56; Spanish and South American influences in, 53–54; use of litany in, 46–48

"FROM A LITANY," 37

"GENERAL," 37

"THE KITE," 21

"NOT DYING," 39

"OUR DEATH," 37

"AN ORDINARY EVENING IN NEW HAVEN," 11–13

"REASONS FOR MOVING," 37

STRAND, MARK, as compared to Stevens, 10–12, 23, 33, 39, 66–68, 73–76; biography of, 14–16; critical analysis of, 83–84; "a mind of winter," 63: symbolist, 25

STEVENS, WALLACE, 63, 80; as compared to Strand, 10–12, 23, 33, 39, 66–68, 73–76; homage to, 10, 59

"THE STORY OF OUR LIVES," 17–32; act of creation, 23; critical analysis of, 17–20; critical views on, 21–32; dehumanizing in, 20; fatal self-consciousness, 31: hopelessness in, 20; ideal state in, 28–31; lack of telos in, 32; narrative reflexivity in 26–28; narrative structure in, 21; questioning of self in, 17; written word as reality in, 25

"TO BEGIN," 24

"THE UNTELLING," 21, 24, 31–32, 55–56

"THE WAY IT IS," 33–41; critical analysis on, 33–36; critical views on, 37–41; movement to public place in, 37–38; perceptions of reality in, 40–41; public phantasmagoria in, 39